<u>The Wife's Secret Weapon!</u>

By

Pastor Steve Morgan

www.ForHimMinistries.net

ISBN-13: 978-0692874455 (For Him Ministries)

ISBN-10: 0692874453

BISAC:
REL105000 Religion >
Sexuality & Gender Studies

TABLE OF CONTENTS

TABLE OF CONTENTS...I

FORWARD...III

ACKNOWLEDGMENTS V

MY TESTIMONY...VII

A MEDIATOR... - 1 -

THE RIGHT BLUEPRINT .... - 6 -

FORGIVENESS ....- 13 -

THE NATURE OF THINGS ....- 21 -

TRUE LOVE...- 34 -

THE RELATOR AND THE WARRIOR..- 39 -

STOP SHOUTING! I CAN'T HEAR YOU. ....- 43 -

WHAT DOES A MAN NEED? ....- 52 -

TAKE THE CHALLENGE!..- 63 -

YOUR ROLE ....- 72 -

MARRIAGE DYNAMICS..- 76 -

    TRUST IS EARNED!...- 78 -

    DICTIONARIES ....- 80 -

    I NEED.... I NEED ....- 82 -

    CUSTOMER SERVICE..- 84 -

    DON'T ASSUME YOU KNOW! ....- 86 -

    INFLUENCING DECISIONS ....- 88 -

    GIVE WHAT YOU'RE GIVEN ....- 97 -

    ARTIFICIAL INTUITION (AI) ....- 99 -

    CHANGING CHANNELS..- 101 -

    TYPES OF AUTHORITY ....- 103 -

    MENOPAUSE ....- 105 -

    TIMING IS EVERYTHING! ....- 108 -

    BOUNDARIES; YOUR PROTECTION! ....- 110 -

    HAVING FUN! ....- 114 -

WHAT ABOUT THE CHILDREN? ....- 117 -

IRON SHARPENS IRON ....- 120 -

CASE STUDIES..- 123 -

FINAL THOUGHTS ....- 147 -

JESUS LOVES YOU!

FORWARD

Ladies, God never intended for you to be frustrated in your marriage. He wants you to be the influential entity He designed you to be. In this book, you will learn of your Secret Weapon and how to use it as God intends. Rest assured, you and your marriage will never be the same.

Marriage really isn't hard. We make it hard because of our misconceptions and the way we go about doing things. But God made it easy as we look into the bible for His answers.

When I first got married, as a Christian, I made it hard on myself because I didn't know what the bible says about this lifestyle. That is why I wrote this book; to help others avoid the same challenges I went through.

If you want to know what Marriage is all about, this book is for you. I will be explaining from a biblical perspective how God designed the man and woman and their unique capabilities. These principles are core abilities given by God and I have proven them to be true in Africa, Honduras, and all over the USA.

If you are a new bride, this book will help you avoid some of the landmines that others have faced.

After reading this book, you will know how to dynamically change the meaning of your marriage into heaven on earth. You will be able to do all this, while having fun.

ACKNOWLEDGMENTS

I have eternal gratitude to my Lord Jesus Christ who is my all in all. To my wife Georgette, who has always supported me in my endeavors; you are my queen. To my daughter Kiliea and son Michael Jr., whom I love very much; my greatest gift to you is what the Lord Jesus Christ has taught me.

There have been some significant men and women of God in my life. This book is possible because of their love, demonstration of Godliness and scriptural knowledge. We all are a summation of our exposures. I am blessed to be exposed to all mentioned here and my encounters with them.
:

- Apostle B. R. Hicks ~ Christ Gospel International, Jeffersonville, Indiana. A mighty woman of God who poured a deep foundation in my life. Thank you for your Labor of Love.

- Bishop Anthony and Pastor Kelly McMillan ~ Pensacola Life Church, Pensacola, Florida. Thank you for your support, encouragement and love; you have become a pillar in my life.

- Apostle Nate and Pastor Valerie Holcomb ~ Christian House of Prayer, Killeen, Texas. Thank you for your ministry, insight, wisdom, understanding and patience.

- Pastor Chris and Nikki Mathis ~ The Summit Church, Crestview, Florida. You have been the Balm of Gilead for my wife and I after a rough work. Thank you for showing us what it looks like to be a Christian and Pastor.

- Pastor Philip Campbell ~ Abundant Life Ministries. You are an anointed leader in the body of Christ and have always been one who reminds me of the need to stay in the spirit of God.

A special thanks to all the couples who allowed me to use them in my study cases. Your transparency has made you real instruments to helping others succeed in their marriage.

Thanks to all who allowed me to use them as a sounding board for clarity while writing this book.

To my sister Candis, who helped me create the book cover… When we were kids, we played a game…Cha Ching Ching!

MY TESTIMONY

My parents were not avid church goers. In fact, the main moral guidance given as a teenager was that I would be in serious trouble if I got any one pregnant.

I saw my mom and dad argue many times. I never saw them sit down and discuss things or resolve problems calmly. My exposure was not of the best way to handle things. It was my salvation with Jesus Christ that embarked me on a journey to development in all aspects of my life.

Much of my knowledge of marriage comes from the bible, some pastors and being married since June 1984. I have learned much from my wife and still do; sometimes from the school of hard knocks.

This book is a result of a question that God asked me. "What do you want from your wife?" I thought I could answer that quickly and discovered that this answer was like an onion; it had many layers. I have been doing personal searches and studying the word of God to discover what I believe are the core needs of a man.

These core needs are universal and I have proven them in several continents. I then sought to find out what role does the wife play in meeting those needs. It is in this research that I ran across what I call the woman's secret weapon. I was surprised to find this Secret Weapon to be so powerful. In fact, a man can know what she is doing and still not be able to or want to resist her. When my wife uses her Secret Weapon on me, I love it and can't get enough! I even find myself wondering when she will do it again!

Pray with me:

Lord, cover me with your blood. Forgive me of my sins; known and unknown according to your word. Open my eyes of understanding. Let me see your word from your perspective and not mine. In Jesus' name I pray, Amen.

1

A MEDIATOR

When a man and a woman marry, the picture is incomplete. An impartial mediator is necessary to help each person to make adjustments that will promote a perfect union. This mediator must be one of authority; one who you revere greater than all things. The best authority is the creator of marriage; God. God's son, Jesus Christ and His directions on marriage gives us a 100% chance for success.

As a person who strives to follow the word of God, I try to disregard how I feel. I find that when I obey the word, things turn out so much better. If I go by my feelings, I just make things worse for myself and others. Following the word of God and the leading of the Holy Ghost is the best way to change a marriage from good to better.

The information in this book is predicated that you have a personal relationship with Jesus Christ. In order to get the results you are looking for, you will need to know Jesus

Christ as your Savior AND Lord. So, let's start from the beginning.

SALVATION

Has anyone ever told you that God loves you and that He has a wonderful plan for your life?

I have a quick, but important question to ask you. God forbid, but if you were to die this second, do you know for sure, beyond a shadow of a doubt, that you would go to Heaven?

Let me quickly share with you what the Holy Bible relays. It reads **"for all have sinned and come short of the glory of God (Romans 3:23)"** and **"for the wages of sin is death, but the gift of God is eternal life through Jesus Christ our Lord (Romans 6:23)"**. The Bible also reads, **"For whosoever shall call upon the name of the Lord shall be saved (Romans 10:13)"**. Would you say that you and I are a "whosoever"? Of course, we are; all of us are.

If you would like to receive the gift God has for you today, say this prayer with your heart and voice out loud.

Dear Lord Jesus, come into my heart, forgive me of my sin. Wash me and cleanse me. Set me Free. Jesus, I thank You that You died for me. I believe that You are the son of God, you died on the cross for my sins and that you rose from the dead to set me free. Fill me with the Holy Ghost. Give me a passion for the lost, a hunger for the things of God, and a holy boldness, to preach the gospel of Jesus Christ. In Jesus' name, I pray, Amen.

Now you can say "I'm Saved: I'm born again, I'm forgiven, and I'm on my way to Heaven, because I have Jesus in my heart!"

As a minister of the gospel of Jesus Christ, I tell you today that all of your sins are forgiven. Always remember to run to God and not from Him because He loves you and has a great plan for your life.

Welcome to the family of God!

Now you have a mediator who will comfort, protect and stick up for you while correcting you. The chances of your marriage being a success have just increased by 100-fold. Congratulations! Your mediator never sleeps and is always there for you. You just call out to Jesus and He will hear you. He will also answer if you just listen with your spirit man.

I can honestly say that Jesus is the mediator that gets all the credit; my wife and I have been married since June 1984. There have been several times when Jesus instructed me to humble myself, and through obedience, He worked it out. You just can't go wrong with an all knowing, all seeing God as your mediator.

To ensure you have a good foundation, I encourage you to read my other books as well:

First Things First (What Every Christian Should Know)

Second Things Second (The Doctrine of Christ)

Now let's look at some principles for your marriage. Like all principles, if you work with them, they will help you and if you violate them, they will hurt you.

YOUR MEDIATOR

Now that you have Jesus as your mediator, he will speak on how you should conduct yourself. He will tell you in the moment what to say, what not to say, what to do and what not to do. He's the one that will tell you to apologize and ask for forgiveness.

Not everything Jesus tells you to do will be easy but, if you deny yourself the right to do or say what you want, you will see your desires come to pass. This is because we are our greatest enemy when it comes to success. This applies to marriage, friendship, business and all other facets of our lives.

In my earlier years of marriage, my wife and I would be at a standoff after an argument. She would not budge nor would I. I remember thinking "I am NOT going to apologize!" Then a small still voice in my heart would reach all the way to my head and say "Yes you are." I knew that it was God on many levels but the first level is: The enemy of marriage will never tell you to apologize; he revels in stubbornness and pride. I had to humble myself and obey God's voice and apologize.

The more I obeyed His voice, the more He spoke to me. I realized that being led by the Holy Ghost is not an accident. It is a purposeful intention to resist all other influences that contradict what He is telling me. These influences are my thoughts and reasoning, my feelings (emotional needs), desires, bodily needs, other people's opinions, society's culture and finally the "everybody is doing it" dogma.

Your mediator wants you to succeed in all facets of your life; to include your marriage. So, His motivation is to see you win! That is why you can trust Him. Jesus is an all knowing, all powerful, omni-present God who will use all to tell you what to do; the outcome will be better than you can imagine. Don't be afraid to be obedient rather leap confidently into your heavenly father's arms. Picture yourself like a child who jumps off the bed into their parent's arms; He will catch you. At first you may need to force yourself to do the right thing and as you are obedient, you will experience a freedom that comes only through doing or saying what is right. The more you practice obedience the more liberty and freedom you will experience. Soon you will run to the obedience corner knowing that your LIFE and LIBERTY comes only from your obedience.

This principle of obedience pertains to every aspect of your life. Jesus wants to liberate your thoughts and give you peace that passes all understanding. He wants to teach you how to speak life and not death to your life as well as others. Jesus will show you how do things that promote peace with yourself and others around you. He is Very interested in what we think, say and do. After all, you are a representative of Him now. You are an ambassador for Jesus Christ on this earth and a witness to heaven of His great love.

2

THE RIGHT
BLUEPRINT

Male or female, we all want the perfect relationship where both partners are fulfilled. It's just that we don't really know how to go about getting it. It's not like we are given a book of instructions on how to assemble this complicated mechanism we call marriage. Or are we?

WHAT BLUEPRINT ARE YOU USING?

When building a house, ONE blueprint is used to ensure that all the plumbing, electrical, air conditioning, rooms and closets work together in a cohesive manner. If more than one blueprint is used, the whole project is destined to fail.

There are two blueprints used in today's society for marriage: the worldly blueprint, and the Godly blueprint. These two blueprints, if mixed, will produce failure. The worldly blueprint was designed by Lucifer (the enemy) to produce failure in marriage.

The Godly blueprint has the power to transform the worst marriage into heaven on earth. Practicing principles out of the Word of God (bible) will fulfill both the husband and wife. God is flawless, His instructions cannot fail. Like my grandmother-in-law used to sing "Well I know my bible is right! Somebody else is wrong."

Our goal in this life is to diligently work on perfecting our ability to apply the Godly blueprint. This is a developmental process; not a quick work. So be patient with yourself and your spouse.

Your best effort is to get back up and try again when you have failed. According to Proverbs, you are considered a just person if you get up and try again. This is important to know: we can begin again when we make mistakes!

Pr 24:16 For a just man falleth seven times, and riseth up again: but the wicked shall fall into mischief.

Notice here that the wicked don't try to stand up. I want to encourage you to keep applying these principles no matter how many times you think you have gotten it wrong; just stand back up and try again. The art of learning is repetition.

Determine today that you are going to use the bible (God's Word) to be your blueprint for how you will conduct yourself with your loved ones from now on. You will find it so much easier. This is Jesus' plan from the beginning! Jesus said in Matthew 11:

Mt 11:28 Come unto me, all [ye] that labour and are heavy laden, and I will give you rest. **29** Take my yoke upon you, and learn of me; for I am meek and lowly in heart: and ye shall find rest unto your souls. **30** For my yoke [is] easy, and my burden is light.

You really can find rest in your marriage by using the bible as your blueprint for marriage.

IF I WERE THE ENEMY!

Marriage is symbolic of Jesus the Groom and His Bride. If I were the enemy, I would try to destroy every resemblance of Jesus and His marriage. Even more importantly, to destroy a marriage that claims Jesus Christ as their Lord would prove that God's word does not work and that He is a liar. Disproving the word of God has been Lucifer's biggest marketing strategy. Satan loves to see people fail in marriage, especially those who profess to have Jesus Christ in their heart.

One of the tricks the enemy uses, is to train up men and women to adopt his failed problem solving skills. It starts by exposing you to the actions of others (your parents or other adults) while you are young to lead you to believe it is acceptable behavior. Naturally, you may repeat what you've seen because this may be all you know. So, the failed technique propagates to the next generation. The enemy does this just to spread worldwide failure in relationships. This is his nature. Jesus described him perfectly in John 10.

Joh 10:10 The thief cometh not, but for to steal, and to kill, and to destroy: I am come that they might have life, and that they might have [it] more abundantly.

The enemy wants to kill all of our dreams, steal all hope away from us and destroy everything that is good in our lives. BUT GOD provides a better solution! I love that Jesus finishes His statement with an opposing solution to the enemy's plan. Abundant Life!

Now that you know that the enemy wants to destroy your marriage and you are aware of his intentions, it should be easier for you to choose the correct blueprint from the designer of marriage; God. He designed marriage to succeed. Actually, I have yet to meet anyone who gets married just to get a divorce.

THE OWNER'S MANUAL

When I take my car to the shop, I try to take it to the manufacturer so that it can be repaired correctly. Most manufacturers that offer customer service train their technicians on the systems that they will be servicing. It may be a little more expensive at the front end, but for the most part, I have saved time and money for not having to deal with rework issues.

In order for me to use an owner's manual of a specific car, I must first own the product that I have the manual for. This is true with the Bible also. Salvation is like possessing a product and once you have it, all the warranties and rights of the owner's manual are legally yours. The Bible is your manual, and if applied and followed properly, it can help you immensely.

If you are going to use the bible as the blueprint for your relationships, then it would be most effective if you received salvation. To do that, go to the first chapter entitled A Mediator and it will lead you through a prayer for salvation.

Once you have prayed and asked Jesus into your heart, you can say "I'm the rightful owner of all warrantees and guarantees, because I have Jesus in my heart!"

Remember! You can stand on this because it says so in the bible. It's not based on how you feel or think about it. It's based on God's pre-established blueprint or owner's manual. The bible says in Romans 10:

Ro 10:9 That if thou shalt confess with thy mouth the Lord Jesus, and shalt believe in thine heart that God hath raised him from the dead, thou shalt be saved. **10** For with the heart man believeth unto righteousness; and with the mouth confession is made unto salvation. **11** For the scripture saith, Whosoever believeth on him shall not be ashamed. **12 ¶** For there is no difference between the Jew and the Greek: for the same Lord over all is rich unto all that call upon him. **13** For whosoever shall call upon the name of the Lord shall be saved.

As a minister of the gospel of Jesus Christ, I tell you today that all of your sins are forgiven. Always remember to **run to God** and not from Him because He loves you and has a great plan for your life.

Welcome to the family of God!

God has made it clear what constitutes salvation. Receiving salvation, entering into the kingdom of heaven, receiving Christ in your heart, and being born again are phrases that the Christian community uses to define joining the Family of God; they're synonymous.

God's word is the measuring stick by which we will be judged on the Day of Judgment so read the bible on a daily basis; even if it is just one line.

I recommend starting with the New Testament first because it is Jesus Christ revealed; the Old Testament is Jesus Christ concealed; many hidden revelations of Him. It's easier to see Jesus in the Old Testament once you are familiar with Him in the New Testament. Also, don't worry about what you don't understand in the bible, if you just work with what you do understand, you will be busy enough. The bible is a living document and the Holy Ghost will make clear to you what you need to understand at that moment.

Prayer: Speak to God daily. Start with Hello Jesus. If you speak to him like you do your best friend, you get so much further in your relationship. Of course, if you must make it difficult, you can put marbles in your mouth and try to speak in the old language. Say something like:

> Lordeth Godeth, I praiseth thee for the wonderfulleth things that thou hast doneth for me. Blesseth me this dayeth Lordeth! Ameneth!! [I'm kidding about this prayer and the marbles]

It is good to thank Jesus for all that He has done and is doing in your life on a regular basis. It's a great prayer.

I always start off with this:

> Lord Jesus, forgive me of my sins that I have committed known and unknown against your word. Thank you for your many blessings that you have given me.

I ask that you …

Take care of ….

Help me to …

Move on my family's behalf.

Bless my Pastor…

Bless my enemies to know you more.

In Jesus Name I pray, Amen.

It is prayer that will help you complete the challenges in this book. I know you will succeed!

Jesus taught us to pray in Matthew 6: 9-15

Mt 6:9 ¶ After this manner therefore pray ye: Our Father which art in heaven, Hallowed be thy name. **10** Thy kingdom come. Thy will be done in earth, as [it is] in heaven. **11** Give us this day our daily bread. **12** And forgive us our debts, as we forgive our debtors. **13** And lead us not into temptation, but deliver us from evil: For thine is the kingdom, and the power, and the glory, for ever. Amen. **14** For if ye forgive men their trespasses, your heavenly Father will also forgive you: **15** But if ye forgive not men their trespasses, neither will your Father forgive your trespasses.

3

FORGIVENESS

The more I share this book with wives; I find that there is a greater issue that prevents women from living in their God ordained position of influence. Taking the challenges in this book opens the door for a dramatic change towards your dream of a great relationship.

Like all great achievements, there are barriers that must be overcome to reach the final goal. When it comes to relationships, a huge barrier is un-forgiveness. I have seen more people induce sickness, cancer and many other ailments to include unhappiness, depression and finally suicide; all because of un-forgiveness. God never designed the human body to shoulder the weight of un-forgiveness.

Most women find it very difficult to touch their spouse when there is a rift or they are angry or harboring resentment towards their husband or others. The sad part is, women are only hurting themselves more when they give in to this type of emotion.

The enemy doesn't want you to press into forgiveness. He knows that if you do, he will lose his persuasive power that he has over you. Please remember that Lucifer, Satan, the Devil, intends to destroy you for now and forever. Telling you that you can forgive but not forget is one of his greatest tricks. Just let it go.

MY TESTAMONY

When I first received Jesus into my heart, I was struggling with getting high. My guilt and condemnation was so much that every sermon I heard seemed to speak against it. I prayed and sought Jesus to help me quit for weeks, when He finally led me to my need to forgive my father. I wanted nothing to do with this subject but I could no longer ignore it. It took me about three months to get my head and heart right to call my father. I told him that I forgave him for the things that he did to me. He replied "I don't know what you are talking about." The next Sunday after church I sat in the same car, in the same seat with the same person that I got high with and when he offered it to me, I thought I was going to throw up! I couldn't do it! Since that time, I have never had a need or a desire to get high again. Praise the Lord!

One of the lessons I have learned here, is that our actions are a product of what is in our heart. The cause is located in our heart. If I fix the cause, the effect will go away. My un-forgiveness of my father was keeping me bound to other sins. Once I forgave my father, regardless of his response, I was set free from an entanglement that I couldn't shake on my own.

This is not about the other person! It's about you getting set free from a very destructive force. Once set free, you can relate with your husband without the influence of un-forgiveness tainting your messages.

THE BENEFITS OF FORGIVENESS

Staying in the state of forgiveness reaps many benefits. It protects us from the spirit of bondage. Forgiveness empowers us to keep His peace. We experience a new sense of hope and joy and are able to live our lives guilt free. The effects that have been difficult to get control of due to un-forgiveness no longer have any strength. Your joy returns, hope and strength is regained and you are free!

GOD'S EXAMPLE

God's plan concerning forgiveness is very clear from Jesus' example and his instructions. Let's take a look at what the bible says.

Mt 18:21 ¶ Then came Peter to him, and said, Lord, how oft shall my brother sin against me, and I forgive him? till seven times? **22** Jesus saith unto him, I say not unto thee, Until seven times: but, Until seventy times seven.

Jesus didn't make this stance to be difficult or challenging. He knew what un-forgiveness does to us and wanted to show us a way out.

If you are a human being, then you have been and/or will be hurt. Some of these incidents may have been imposed upon you with no fault of your own. A trust that was betrayed, verbal abuse, physical abuse, molestation, rape and many other forms of offense can affect us to our core being.

Regardless of what we have experienced, it is within our power to choose to forgive. Forgiveness is the first step to complete healing in your body, soul and spirit.

Mt 6:14 For if ye forgive men their trespasses, your heavenly Father will also forgive you: **15** But if ye forgive not men their trespasses, neither will your Father forgive your trespasses.

Even the Lord 's Prayer includes "Forgive us our trespasses as we forgive those who trespass against us".

You should now understand why I say that you must forgive ALL who have hurt you. It is for your benefit that you forgive.

YOU MUST DECIDE TO FORGIVE FOR YOUR SAKE!

Forgiveness is not an emotion; it is a deliberate act on your part; a decision. If forgiveness is a feeling, then I wonder what Jesus felt when he was beaten and hung on the cross. In fact, while hanging on the cross, in the middle of his gasps for air, he said:

Lu 23:34 Then said Jesus, Father, forgive them; for they know not what they do. And they parted his raiment, and cast lots.

One of the questions I ask myself before I justify holding a grudge is "Have I been treated worse than the crucifixion of my Lord Jesus?" My answer is always "NO". Therefore, I am obligated to forgive.

FORGET ABOUT IT

To what degree are we to forgive? Let's look at God's example of forgiveness:

Jer 31:34 And they shall teach no more every man his neighbour, and every man his brother, saying, Know the LORD: for they shall all know me, from the least of them unto the greatest of them, saith the LORD: for **I will forgive their iniquity, and I will remember their sin no more.**

Forgetting about something done to you is not suggesting that we practice selective amnesia, it is the practice of not allowing your memories to persuade you to do anything contrary to the word of God. For example:

Jas 4:17 Therefore to him that knoweth to do good, and doeth [it] not, to him it is sin.

Notice that this is not predicated on whether someone hurt you.

THE PROCESS OF FORGIVING

In order for you to start the process of forgiveness, you must begin by speaking it with your voice. Read aloud the prayer that Jesus said to pray:

Matthew 6:10 After this manner therefore pray ye: Our Father which art in heaven, Hallowed be thy name. **10** Thy kingdom come. Thy will be done in earth, as it is in heaven. **11** Give us this day our daily bread. **12** And forgive us our debts, as we forgive our debtors. **13** And lead us not into temptation, but deliver us from evil: For thine is the kingdom, and the power, and the glory, forever. Amen. **14** For if ye forgive men their trespasses, your heavenly Father will also forgive you: **15** But if ye forgive not men their trespasses, neither will your Father forgive your trespasses.

Right now! I want you to say "I forgive (the person that hurt you) and I forgive myself". If you find it difficult to say it for the first time then you are definitely working on the right issue. Once you have said it once, you must say it several times more and then every day until there is no emotional connection left.

Once you start the process of forgiveness, your Father in heaven forgives you. The bondage of un-forgiveness will fall off of you like autumn leaves. You will begin to experience the joy and freedom you were intended to live.

With this barrier removed, you now have the Grace to continue with these challenges and reap the benefits. You are more than a conqueror... So, start changing your destiny!

Notice that Jesus directs us to pray "Thy will be done in earth, as it is in heaven"? It is His intention to start heaven in you right now. This is how heaven comes to earth. He does it by bringing heaven in your life right now.

I know that some of the subjects in this book are difficult. But if you hang in there, I guarantee that Jesus will move on your behalf and perform miracles beyond your expectations.

Eph 3:20 Now unto him that is able to do exceeding abundantly above all that we ask or think, according to the power that worketh in us,

Let Jesus be the power that works in you and through you!

Forgiveness is a powerful weapon against the snares of the enemy. Do not under estimate how the enemy will try to influence you to keep an issue with someone. You will hear all sorts of justifications, in your thoughts and from others, to hold a grudge. God could have done the same to us; instead He died on the Cross. It didn't feel good but it was necessary. Forgiving may be difficult, but it is necessary.

It is my experience that forgiving others is not for them but for me. Doctors have confirmed that biologically, it is unhealthy to harbor ill will against someone. When I forgive someone, I release the pressures off of my life. I am willing to believe that Jesus has our joy in mind when he stresses the need to forgive.

I am reminded of a woman who the Holy Ghost revealed to me that she was harboring un-forgiveness against a man who physically abused her. As I prayed for her, the Lord led me to insist that she speak out that she forgives him. She struggled and strained to frame the words and finally she said them. It was clear that these were the hardest words that she had ever had to speak. Once she succeeded, a spirit of relief came over her and she wept in ecstasy as the Holy Ghost began to pour into her and minister to her needs. She was truly set free that day!

God is very interested in our ability to get along with others. To the point that Jesus gave these instructions:

Matt 5:23 Therefore if thou bring thy gift to the altar, and there rememberest that thy brother hath ought against thee; **24** Leave there thy gift before the altar, and go thy way; first be reconciled to thy brother, and then come and offer thy gift.

Let's be diligent at keeping un-forgiveness out of our heart!

When we forgive, we win and the testimony of Christ wins! Let's stay in the WIN – WIN business!

You must then bless the one you are forgiving. Jesus said:

Mt 5:44 But I say unto you, Love your enemies, bless them that curse you, do good to them that hate you, and pray for them which despitefully use you, and persecute you;

Your success in getting free of the bondage of un-forgiveness is hinged on whether you learn to forgive AND pray for those who have offended you.

Whatever wrong that has been done to you from whomever, past or present, you must choose to forgive. It is your only way out of the bondage.

HOW DO I FORGIVE?

1. Choose to forgive
2. Speak out your forgiveness aloud often
3. Bless the one you are forgiving in prayer

Here is an example prayer:

Lord Jesus, forgive me of all my sins, known and unknown according to your word. Help me to stay in forgiveness as you forgive me. I forgive (name). Now I bless (name) and pray that you touch them and move on their behalf for your cause.

YOU CAN DO THIS!!!

Php 4:13 I can do all things through Christ which strengtheneth me.

4

THE NATURE OF
THINGS

Now that we are using the bible to determine how we operate in our marriage, let's look at some revelatory information about men and women.

Through some study, I have found that the Hebrew word for Name can be translated as Nature. So when we examine the Hebrew definition of a name, we are looking into the nature of that being. So let's look at some Hebrew definitions.

When we look up the Hebrew definition for the words Man, Dominion, Created, Male and Female, we see a unique picture into the order of Gods Plan.

Gen 1:26 ¶ And God said, Let us make **man** in our image, after our likeness: and let them have **dominion** over the fish of the sea, and over the fowl of the air, and over the cattle, and over all the earth, and over every creeping thing that creepeth upon the earth.

The Hebrew definition for **Man** is אדם adam (pronounced *aw-dawm')* meaning: Mankind

All of mankind was called Man and Man was to have Dominion over the earth. The Hebrew definition for **Dominion** follows:

Dominion - רדה radah (pronounced raw-daw')

    1) Rule

    2) Dominion

    3) Take

    4) Prevaileth

    5) Reign

    6) Ruler

    7) Tread down

    8) Subjugate

Mankind has been assigned to dominate the earth which was delegated by God. Please note that this is not divided among gender; rather given to all of Mankind.

Gen 1:27 So God **created** man in his own image, in the image of God created he him; **male** and **female** created he them.

Here we see that God in his infinite wisdom and balance created a balanced creature called Mankind. Mankind was **created** which means:

Hebrew - Meaning:

Created - ברא bara' (pronounced baw-raw')

1) Shaped, Formed or Fashioned

2) To be Chosen

3) Dispatched

4) Made Fat

When God created mankind, he shaped him in balance as a combination of male and female. This is before the female was drawn from the rib. Here is a perfect picture of God in his perfect balance. As one, the male and female influence was destined to have dominion over all the earth; just as God has dominion over the heavens. God shaped, formed and fashioned us in His image, chose us, dispatched us and made us fat (or gave us the equipment) to do the assignment given. We have all that we need to succeed.

God has delegated His authority for dominance on the earth to Mankind. He does not interfere unless we request His intervention. You see, unlike some bosses we have worked for, who micro-manage your job, God will not micro-manage. This is why mankind must ask God for guidance and help, so that we can give God the liberty to work on the earth.

Now we know that the mission for Male and Female is the same, we can look at the differences to determine how each goes about accomplishing the same task.

MALE AND FEMALE

When God created mankind, he did not design them to hold or contain stress. He designed a relief mechanism that allows Mankind to vent stress successfully for better health. When God physically separated the male and female, the method of venting stress was split in two. Let's now look at how each deal with stress after the separation.

MALE

In Hebrew, the word "name" means nature. It should be no surprise that the Hebrew definition of **Male** is זכר zakawr meaning male gender of mankind. However, its root word sheds some light on the nature of the male:

> Root word to **Male** - זכר zakar (pronounced zaw-kar')

> 1) To Remember
> 2) Think
> 3) To mention

I would also like to add some additional traits here.

> Warrior
> Conqueror
> Protector
> Contemplator

This is not to say that the female does not remember things or that she does not think or mention things. This is simply to point out that males deal with stress differently. When a male is dealing with issues, he most likely is going to become "quieter" than usual. Men do not usually talk about issues to deal with stress. The male needs to process by thinking about the issue until he is relieved of the stress. Once he accomplishes this, he will most likely share with his spouse the issue. Mind you ladies, this could take days, weeks and even months. Be patient! Men get relief from stress when they can think it through. This is very therapeutic for us as our proclivity is to get relief by thinking about it. If a man is unable to think about an issue, he can't find relief from the pressure and will eventually seek means to get relief.

With this understanding, ladies, when your husband seems to be more distant, don't assume he is angry with you.

I would also like to point out some additional strengths of the Male; he is primarily visually stimulated. He is very keen to your touch as well. He is not verbally stimulated as much as the female.

FEMALE

As with the male, the Hebrew definition for **Female** is of no surprise:

> Meaning: נְקֵבָה neqebah (pronounced nek-ay-baw') meaning female, woman
>
>> The root word also sheds some light on the subject:
>>
>> Meaning: נָקַב naqab (pronounced naw-kab')
>>
>> 1) Expressed
>>
>> 2) Pierce Through
>>
>> 3) Appoint

Additional study has shown that the female has additional strengths:

Nurturer

Nester

Relational

Like the male, the female was designed to deal with stress, but differently. When a female is stressed, she gets relief by expressing the issue. Her success in dealing with the stress is very high when she can express it to another person. Like men, once the stress has been dealt with, she can press on with other matters stress free. Women get relief from stress by discussing it.

When women have problems, they are more apt to talk about it. When they talk about it, they get the same relief as men do when they think about it. In fact, women don't need a solution most of the time; the act of expressing it actually sheds the pressure like taking off a raincoat.

I would like to point out that men think the same way women express it when it comes to dealing with stress; it's just that they don't verbalize it. If a man wrote down on a white board all the things he thinks when he is dealing with stress, and a woman wrote all the things she says on a white board, you would find that both sides look similar. This is why men must learn to wipe the board clean after listening to his wife; just as he does with his thoughts once relieved of stress.

One way ladies can help with this process is tell them what you need up front before you start de-stressing. This helps him know what is expected and he will gladly comply. If you need him to be a good listener, tell him. If you are looking for some advice, ask him for it and tell him that you want to explain the situation completely first.

One way to know if your man is confused on the role he needs to play is when you want him to be a listener and he starts giving you advice. Don't expect people to read your mind; tell them what you need.

One way husbands can stay on top of which role to play is if the wife forgets to inform them what is needed, he can simply ask: "Do you want my advice or are you in need of a good listener?"

Now that we know how each gender manages stress, let's be understanding of each other's processes and not force our methodology on each other. A typical comment from a woman to a man might be "why don't you just talk to me? You will feel better." She is unknowingly asking the man to change his nature to a female's. This only frustrates the male. On the other hand, the man might say, "why do you keep talking about the negative things? Can't you just let it go?" He is unknowingly asking her to be a man. This frustrates the woman.

I cannot stress this enough! It is very dangerous for a marriage to deny a specific nature to relieve itself from stress. The male should never ask the female to be a male (Don't express it until you have thought about it for a long while). Incidentally, if the man listens long enough, he will hear his wife give the solution that he was thinking. Likewise, the female should never ask the male to be a female (Talk to me!). Most men will talk about it once they get it figured out. Let's be patient enough to allow each other to process completely without the added pressure to do something against our nature.

LET'S MUDDY THE WATER

Now that I have given you the core functionality of the male and female, please be aware that there are various levels at which each operate. Some men will talk sooner than others and some women will refrain from talking more than others. This does not change what your core need is for stress relief. I'm only validating that there are more variables that will contribute to the level in which you operate. Some of these variables are: your temperament, your experiences, the culture you grew up in and several others.

Another factor to consider: the intensity of the stress will influence the amount of their core need to be satisfied. Some examples; an expresser may become quiet while mourning a lost love one. A contemplator may begin to chat over an upcoming event to relieve stress. Use this information loosely to allow your spouse to respond to dramatic moments in their own way. Patience is the most important tool here.

My advice to you is to apply the core fundamentals strictly speaking and allow your mate to vary it as they need. After some practice, you will learn the personal needs of your spouse.

YOU ARE THE ACCELEROMETER

In science, many instruments are used for quantifying measurements. There is a specific instrument we all have in common. It is the accelerometer.

The accelerometer does not sense consistency. It is only capable of sensing change. Aren't we just like that? We can ride in a car that keeps a steady direction and speed and we feel as if we are standing still. Just as soon as the car begins to turn or change speed, we sense the change. The stronger the change the more we are made aware of it. This is the purpose of this book. Ladies, I am asking you to take the challenges to expose your husband to some significant changes. Trust me when I say that you will get his undivided attention and drive him crazy with the need to understand where you are coming from. At the same time, you are going to have a blast because I will be telling you what he is thinking when you do the challenges.

THE POWER OF CHANGE IS FOR <u>YOUR</u> CHANGE

One of the biggest stumbling blocks in a relationship is when one person tries to change the other. Most of the time, the thing you are trying to change is an effect, not a cause. Only God knows why a person is doing something. He has to fix the cause in order for the change to be permanent.

HOWEVER! The only power we have is to change ourselves. You and God can work on the causes of your life to affect permanent change. You are responsible for accepting your spouse for who they are right now. You must work on changing you; not your spouse. It is in your change that will improve your relationship. When you change, in time, it will provoke a change in your spouse.

THE DANGER OF TESTS

I once was obsessing over who would do the dishes first. I would not do them to test my wife to see if she would do them. If she did not, then she failed my test and then I would become angry with her. These types of tests are unfair. We expect that our subject should know the rules of our test without our explanation. Before we justify our tests, let me ask you if you have ever been mentally or physically occupied that you did not notice the dishes or something else. EVERYONE has moments of being preoccupied to the point they are not as alert as other times. In the house especially, the home should be a place of safety to allow for such things. A home is a safe refuge from a demanding world. Why would we be so insensitive as to make the home anything less? Don't put people to the test. Give them rest!

LISTEN AT THE PITCH OF YOUR VOICE

One of the reasons the German language is considered very harsh is because they do not speak with intonation (change the pitch of their voice). It takes some effort for a German to learn English for this very reason. Learning the purpose of pitch can be a valuable tool to help you convey what you really mean.

When we greet someone, we instinctively raise the pitch of our voice; especially if we like them. Most of the time, the raised pitch is interpreted as excitement in seeing them and is considered a complement. We in turn would most likely raise our pitch without realizing it.

In most cases, the deeper the natural voice, the more one is likely to be misunderstood. I have a low pitch voice and it is naturally loud. My wife did not grow up around a lot of men and has occasionally perceived that I am upset when I am not. After several years of trying to figure out the cause of this misunderstanding, I realized that I would get a more positive result when I raised the tone of my voice just a bit. She then hears my message over the tone of my voice.

Try to practice changing the tone of your voice when you speak to someone and see the results you get. The balance to this is if you have a very high pitched voice, you might want to practice lowering the tone of you voice for better effect. I would recommend asking a friend for their opinion on your voice, and test the changes to see if you are getting the results that you desire. Besides, it might be fun to experiment with your friends.

WHO IS GOING TO TEACH YOUR HUSBAND?

1 Peter 3:7 Likewise, ye husbands, **dwell with them according to knowledge**, giving honour unto the wife, as unto the weaker vessel, and as being heirs together of the grace of life; that your prayers be not hindered.

What knowledge is Peter referring? The simple answer is the knowledge YOU teach him. I believe within your nature is the information he needs to succeed in your relationship. However, he will not be able to receive it unless you deliver it with your Secret Weapon. The things you need to share must enter his heart; not his head. The Secret Weapon gives you direct access to his heart. Anything you deposit into his heart will change him dramatically. Anything you put into his head will be logically analyzed and sometimes dismissed; not that logic is a bad thing. It's just that you are dealing with him on a relational level; this level is higher than logic and can only be dealt with by the heart.

My wife and I have had several conversations concerning my tone. Finally, I was able to share with her how I felt about this situation. I told her:

> A married couple will be more vulnerable to each other than other family and friends. This can make us more sensitive to each other. With that said, I need you to walk me through the times you hear a tone. I do not hear tones. If you cut our conversation off, then I will surely do it again because I don't get it.

> This is like the time my dad told me to wipe that look off my face and then he balled his fist and punched me in the face. I was nine years old and the only thing I felt was fear so I don't know what my face looked like... it sure wasn't defiance or disrespect. Maybe if he had said "Michael, I don't like it when you are frowning...it makes me think you are being disrespectful", then I would have known how to avoid getting punched the next time. Instead, I was vulnerable to his interpretation of something; to this day I have no idea what it is.

> Do you like me being vulnerable to your interpretation with me having no idea? If not, then you must walk me through your definition of tones. When you hear one... use it as a teaching opportunity right then and there. This is the only way I know of how to fix this.

Much to my wife's credit, she agreed to try to teach me.

PRINCIPLE: Being right and delivering your point incorrectly is just as bad as being wrong.

You will get the same results as being wrong when you poorly deliver a right message. Ladies, here is where your Secret Weapon makes your presentation right.

Try starting off your conversations by telling your spouse your desired outcome. Maybe something like "I want us both to be satisfied with the outcome of our conversation. Here are my concerns..." And finally finish it off with "How do you see this and what ideas do you have for a compromise?" One of the biggest lessons I have learned is that my wife can be standing right next to me and still see something different.

It isn't always about who is right or wrong; sometimes it is about what makes you both happy.

SIDE NOTE: (Right and Wrong)

Please don't get caught up in the "who is right or who is wrong" mentality. This is a guarantee that you will never get past this obstacle. There is a higher order of thought that we must strive to achieve. It is the idea that being wrong is essential to discovering new truths about ourselves, our spouse, our children, our co-workers and our friends. It's an opportunity to learn some conditional facet that has never come up before. Being wrong isn't the only way to learn but it is just as essential as being right.

5

TRUE LOVE

When I think of true love, I think of Jesus Christ. He said in John 15:13:

John 15:13 Greater love hath no man than this, that a man lay down his life for his friends.

When we say that we love someone, do we mean that we will lay our lives down for that person? It is with this reckless abandonment of self that we find a force that knows no bounds; True Love.

You may have been taught that sex is Love, then you will need to study the true definition of True Love. I find 1Corinthians 13:1-7 to be an accurate account of perfect love. Notice that sex is not mentioned here.

1 Cor 13:1 Though I speak with the tongues of men and of angels, and have not love, I am become as sounding brass, or a tinkling cymbal. **2** And though I have the gift of prophecy, and understand all mysteries, and all knowledge;

and though I have all faith, so that I could remove mountains, and have not love, I am nothing. **3** And though I bestow all my goods to feed the poor, and though I give my body to be burned, and have not love, it profiteth me nothing. **4** ¶ Love suffereth long, and is kind; love envieth not; love vaunteth not itself, is not puffed up, **5** Doth not behave itself unseemly, seeketh not her own, is not easily provoked, thinketh no evil; **6** Rejoiceth not in iniquity, but rejoiceth in the truth; **7** Beareth all things, believeth all things, hopeth all things, endureth all things. **8** ¶ Love never faileth: but whether there be prophecies, they shall fail; whether there be tongues, they shall cease; whether there be knowledge, it shall vanish away.

The word Love in John 15:13 and Charity in 1Corinthians 13:1 have the same meaning in the Greek. Which is $\alpha\gamma\alpha\pi\eta$ agape (pronounced ag-ah'-pay) meaning brotherly love.

When Jesus suffered many things, died and rose again to be with the Father in heaven, He introduced a new concept to the Greeks. Until then, there wasn't a word to describe the sacrificial love that Jesus gave for mankind. This is when the word Agape was created, which encapsulated a selfless disregard for the betterment of all others.

If you were to ask God why he loves you, He will not mention a physical attribute as a reason. God loves you because He does. Nothing you do or say will change His love for you. Think about it. If I say that I love you because you have a nice body, then when the body grows old, the love will also. My wife asked me why I loved her and I replied "I don't know. I just do". Later I learned this principle which made me feel great because I didn't need a reason to love her.

Please don't be hard on someone who gives a list of why they love you. They may feel pressured to qualify their love for you because of your question. They may not know this principle that love just loves for no reason at all. The best thing to do is tell them that you love them and that you can't explain it; you just don't know why.

LOVE IS NOT A FEELING! IT IS A COMMITMENT

Love is a commitment! Emotional "warm fuzzies" come and go but a real commitment will endure sacrifice. This is why the scriptures state that God loves us so much that He gave His only begotten son (Jesus Christ) so that we could live. As a father, I don't think that I could give my son away. Yet, God did it for us. This is a painful sacrifice for any father. Jesus suffered many things to fulfill the punishment of sin. All because of his love for us. He knew that He was going to suffer and did not stray away from His commitment towards us. Jesus loves us so much that nothing could stop Him from fulfilling His commitment to suffer for us. Love is not a feeling…It is a commitment!

Love doesn't always feel good; it is not always convenient or easy. Love is a commitment. So, commit to it whole heartily. Stop holding back!

MY TESTAMONY

There was a time in my marriage that I was seriously considering throwing in the towel. I was frustrated and wanted to get some relief. One day during prayer, God confronted me with the question "what do I want?" My answer to the question caught me by surprise; I wanted my marriage to work. Next the Lord asked me "Then why are you contradicting yourself?" He made it obvious to me that I was contradicting myself. My actions and heart were not lining up with my own desire. It was clear to me then; I was to act like I love my wife regardless of how I feel or how she responded. The focus was that I could not contradict myself for any reason.

I committed to love my wife and stop holding back. I would not allow myself to use the excuse of her actions or inactions to influence as to how I was going to respond. Surprisingly enough, I was liberated from the frustration of contradicting myself. I realized then that my peace is centered on my actions and whether they agree with my heart or not. This was such a relief that I began to respond to her according to my own heart and not her behavior.

The better I get at following my own heart, the easier life gets for me. This has also provoked a change in my wife's behavior as well.

NOTE! I do not condone physical violence. If this exists, you must physically separate yourself from the situation and insist on counseling.

Ladies, you don't like to be treated harshly by your husbands. I get it. But the greatest offense you can endure is when you allow your husband to dictate how you are going to love him. Trust me on this one... Stop contradicting yourself! There is great peace when your words and actions agree with your heart.

If you are dealing with emotional abuse, read this book and do the challenges (I know what I'm suggesting is difficult). Then after the challenges, you tell him that you would like him to read some information you have for him (with your Secret Weapon). (The information is my book, The Husband's Toolbox.) He will most likely be compelled to read it because of the core needs you have met. Like you, I will teach him how to meet your core needs.

The influence is on your side of the court now. You have a huge advantage over him. Once you start the challenges you will see what I'm talking about.

OK! You're probably thinking "My husband is not going to read a book written by a man on how to treat his wife!" Don't be so sure. If you do as much of the challenges as physically possible; you will be surprised at what he would be willing to do for you.

6

THE RELATOR AND
THE WARRIOR

Ladies, have you ever said something to your husband and he acts like he didn't even hear you? Hmmm, why is that?

Remember earlier I said the men are not verbally stimulated? You are! A woman can be performing all sorts of tasks with plenty of noise going on and someone can enter the area and say something totally off subject and she will hear clearly what was said. This is because women are verbally stimulated. You have such a heightened awareness for speech, you naturally tune to it immediately. Just like when a doctor takes a rubber mallet and hits your knee and you kick your leg involuntarily. It is your reflex. This is because God made you an expresser.

You are also a relater! Is it any wonder why you want to develop relationships and feel that talking things out draws you closer to someone? The truth is, you are right. When two people can talk things over, they will become more entwined with each other. The relationship is stronger.

I believe God put in you the need to discuss things and to develop relationships to include your husband. The challenge is that he is not verbally stimulated, an expresser, nor is he a relator. If you treat him as if he is verbally stimulated, you will become frustrated over your failed attempts to communicate.

Men are warriors. They thrive on winning and success. They are built for the battle field and they have a reflex of their own. You see, men need to be able to ward off attacks and aggressive behavior. This is why God equipped them with what I call the wall. Yes, the wall has come between many a foe to allow the man to continue on with his daily business unscathed. Just as women are unaware of how keenly they pick up conversation, the man is unaware of how quickly his wall is deployed. Both are, what I call, a natural reflex. Try to be understanding if your husband treats you like you are a warrior. We (men and women) have a proclivity to think we all function the same as us.

Ladies, this is why you think your husband is not a human being. He won't respond like one when you speak to him. You're not even sure he understands plain English! The truth is, you are being confronted with the wall.

Here are some signs that you have hit the wall:

>You ask him to do something and he forgets.

>You say something that would provoke a reasonable answer from a human being and you don't get one.

He does something once but doesn't maintain it.

He comes into the conversation well after it started.

His comments clearly tell you he is not listening.

He only does something after you have approached him many times and then he stops doing it.

He seems insensitive to you.

He seems uncompassionate to you.

He seems disconnected.

You get into an argument at night and he can still get some rest.

There are so many signs of you hitting the wall that I am just going to use these as a general idea of what you are facing.

As a warrior, men cannot allow their emotions to get involved while in battle; some professors of war say that people who engage in combat mentally shut down to a primal mode of thinking. Without the wall, it would ensure defeat and the greater cause would be defenseless. This is why the wall is so necessary.

WHAT CAUSES THE WALL TO ACTIVATE?

Activating your husband's wall can occur with the smallest peep of your voice or only when you start shouting. It can also be activated when there is tension between the two of you. It differs from man to man and the circumstances. It does not mean that he's unwilling to listen, it just means the wall was activated accidentally or on purpose for defensive reasons. Remember that this is purely a reflex and most men are unaware that they have this wall. He has had it all his life and it is normal to him.

I believe that signs of the wall occur at a very young age. When a mother has to repeat herself to her son; this is a good sign of the wall being present.

BUT THERE IS HOPE!

Once the wall is activated you still have what it takes to get around it. Your Secret Weapon can circumvent the powers of his wall in a microsecond. The best thing is; he will like it!

Fortunately, not only did God create us with the ability to deal with stress, he designed men with a weak spot that only his wife can use to get past the wall and into his heart. Yes, you can crack that shell with the greatest of ease with your Secret Weapon. This Weapon is provided by God and you already have it. Read the next chapter to find out about your Secret Weapon!

7

STOP SHOUTING!
I can't hear you.
(The Secret Weapon)

In many countries, the culture today is to speak up! Be heard! Voice your opinion! Be the loudest voice in the room! Make a stand!

We are also duped to believe that we are getting our message across to the person when we are shouting. Nothing could be further from the truth. Fact is, the louder you get, the less people listen.

Many might tell you that you are not getting your point across because you take too many rabbit trails and the listener gets lost in your sentence. Maybe you could be more direct but that is no guarantee that you will be heard.

The loudest person in a public argument will always be viewed by others as the one in the wrong. When a married couple argues in public, they dishonor one another. If the husband is shouting, he presents himself to the public as an insensitive husband that no woman would ever want. If the wife is shouting in public, she is viewed as a brute and sympathy will go towards the husband. Eventually, each will be hurt by how they were humiliated. When an issue arises in public that could escalate to an argument, tell your spouse that you can discuss this later. Remember, children fight in public.

I want to share with you a secret that will have your husband not only listen to you but allow you to express it the way you always do.

If you are a woman and want to know how to get your message through to your husband, keep reading. The solution to this puzzle seems to have been lost over the generations. The techniques here will work anytime you have a female to male interaction; regardless if it is a wife to a husband, a mother to a son, a sister to a brother or a daughter to a father. After reading this book, you should be able to get better responses from him and regain your peace of mind. Your success here will make for a happier home for all involved. You will be glad you took these challenges!

Ladies, most likely, your frustration in trying to communicate with males stems from you trying to use the wrong tool for the job. You can't communicate with men like you can with your girlfriend. Worse, many women take advice on how to communicate with men from other women. Come on ladies, you go to a hair dresser to tell you how to take care of your hair. You have an auto repairman fix your car. You may even get decorating advice from an interior designer. Why not get advice on how to deal with men from a man who will give you Godly counsel!

So, I decided to help you with this subject from a biblical and man's perspective. The male that you would like to improve your relationship with will agree with me on what works. There are some differences and I will always recommend asking them what they prefer. But for the most part, 99% of the men I have shared these principles with have agreed that they are true.

God gave you your Secret Weapon so that you could get past your husband's wall with the greatest of ease. In fact, it's so simple, that you will be tempted to stop reading this book. BUT WAIT!!! I'm going to show you how to use it to its fullest extent and tell you why it works.

Your Secret Weapon comes from Proverbs 15:

Pr 15:1 ¶ A soft answer turneth away wrath: but grievous words stir up anger.

Your Secret Weapon is a gentle touch with a whisper. I'm not kidding! Men cannot defend against it. In fact, we are drawn to it like a moth to a flame. We just can't get enough.

So why is a gentle touch and a whisper so effective? Because it satisfies a core male need... We need to be accepted. Let's look at this closer.

A GENTLE TOUCH

We men are warriors, conquerors and confronters. In the field of battle a man uses all his senses to stay apprised of his surroundings as well as the conflict before him. If an enemy were to graze him on the leg, his gift of being physically stimulated would allow him to counter the attacker before he could visually see him. When you gently touch your husband, you heighten his awareness and gain his full attention. We men are physically and visually stimulated as much as you are verbally stimulated. So, when you gently touch your husband, it alerts him mentally that something important is about to take place.

Isn't it interesting that the first response of most women when they are frustrated is to withhold touching their husbands? You can learn to ignore this type of "gag reflex" to successfully resolve the issues in your favor by gently touching him and whispering what you have to say.

So now that you have his undivided attention by touching him and you understand why this is so important for you, tell him something in a whisper.

A WHISPER

Secrets are intriguing. If you want to get someone's attention, you can start whispering and they will strain themselves to hear the mystery. It is more interesting to hear a thing in a whisper than any other way of communicating. When you see someone whisper, do you ever find yourself wondering what is being said?

We all want to be included and feel wanted. When someone whispers to you, they are including you. Whispering is a very personal invitation into the whisperer's life. Whispering also requires that two or more people come closer than they would in normal communication. Personal space is usually intruded upon and allowed for a whisper.

I once had a teacher in High School who would whisper to get everyone's attention. Much to my surprise, it worked every time. It helped that the message was never the same. Make sure that your whispering is not only when you are angry. Vary the messages so that the listener is intrigued to hear what you are about to say.

Pr 15:1 ¶ A soft answer turneth away wrath: but grievous words stir up anger.

When you whisper, you are telling him that you are including him in your life and he can't resist that. The whisper also does not trigger the wall so you now have access straight into his heart. He will respond to you like a real human being. You will be surprised how effective this is! One more scripture to give you an idea of the power of a whisper:

Pr 25:15 ¶ By long forbearing is a prince persuaded, and a soft tongue breaketh the bone.

TESTAMONY

I was pastoring a church for a pastor who was deployed for three months. While working there, a couple came to me for counseling. The husband was an introvert and the woman was an extravert and loud. She was so frustrated that she would do anything to resolve the issue. After listening to her for a few minutes I stopped her and asked her if she would like to go on a challenge with me. She agreed so I laid out the ground rules.

I told her that she could not use her voice to her husband for two weeks. She could use it towards her family and friends but not her husband. If he asked her to repeat it, then she was to get closer. If it was time for dinner, she would have to go to him and whisper it.

After the first week, she came to church beaming, smiling like a possum. Noticing the dramatic change in her countenance, I asked her how things were going and she said "Great"! So, I asked her how so? She confided in me and said "I have been able to tell my husband in a five-minute conversation whispering what I have tried to tell him with my voice for the last three years". She said the same things to him and he could hear it and responded in such a way that let her know he understood. The softer and quieter she got the more he was able to listened to her and the easier it was for her to touch his heart. She stopped triggering the wall!

Most men are familiar with confrontation. We practice it from youth up playing cowboys and Indians, good versus evil, or fighting with swords. Once the conflict is over, we go back to our daily routine without a hitch; for the most part. This is why we can go to sleep and get a good night's rest after an argument. Additionally, there is something inside every man designed to protect our family and stand for what is right. Unfortunately, it may manifest in an unbalanced or inappropriate way. Regardless of how hard the male appears, he has a weakness that he cannot deny or withstand.

In all the weapons of warfare God equipped male, he left a defenseless spot that can only be pierced by his love's whisper and gentle touch. We have no defense against our wife's soft touch with a whisper. When properly given by his wife, it will keep him up at night and provoke a change in him. In other words, you will be the one getting the rest at night while he tosses and turns.

I didn't say that this would be easy!!!! Your biggest persuasion comes with the soft touch AND a whisper. For the important things that require clear communication, you need to get through to him. You must resist the urge to fight or approach him like a man and gently touch him and whisper what you want from him. It will reduce your frustration level by a hundred-fold. You can say the same words you would have said in a shout and he will respond to you in a surprisingly different manner.

You know that you have mastered this technique when you get quieter when you get angry. Just whispering the same words, you would have shouted, can be the difference of the results you desire versus a fruitless argument. Just remember to use the gentle touch and whispering to love as well.

OK, some may say that this is not going to work. Let me ask you first, what do you want the most? Do you want results or do you want the pleasure of shouting at him? Very rarely will you get both. If you want results, then you must deny your trained normal way of responding. If you want to shout, then you will be at this same subject again in the future. You can bank on that!

I want to encourage you that you can change!

<u>TROPHIES</u>

Men LOVE trophies, it is a sign that they have succeeded. A conquer never tires of winning. Each trophy has a significant memory of him getting it right and rising above the rest. A warrior who never wins a battle will eventually stop fighting and surrender to his enemy.

Ladies, you have a trophy that you can award him that is coveted by your husband. Don't underestimate his need to win with you; it is very powerful force!

Just like a trophy, your trophy has several parts. Your trophy consists of your arms around him, look him in the eye, whisper to him that you really appreciate what he has done. Finally, give him a warm, meaningful kiss. No one likes a partial trophy. So, make sure you give him a completely assembled trophy.

Yes, to you it may not mean the same but to him, it means that he did good by you. It also encourages him to do it again. Why, because he desperately needs to know that he is successful with you. A trophy from you is an unmistakable sign to him that he can do a certain thing and win with you. Ladies, trust me on this one! He will go for the trophy every time!

When my wife gives me a trophy, I store what I did in the stronghold of my mind so that I can remember to do it again. If I don't get a trophy, then what I did wasn't really what she wanted; so, I forget about it.

If you see your husband trying different things with you, he is searching for the trophy. Why not make it easier on you and him? Use your Secret Weapon, tell him what you want and give him a trophy when he attempts to do it. Notice I said attempts? If you want him to keep going in that direction, you have to encourage him; trophies will never fail you.

It's a win-win situation! He never gets tired of the trophies and you teach him to repeat the things you like! If a man knows he can win, he will always engage in the game just to get a trophy!

Have fun! Giving a trophy for a failed effort in the right direction is very powerful. You can say to him after the trophy, "honey, next time, I like red roses better and one will do." He won't forget that!!! You can even be laughing when you do it, the trophy disarms his defensiveness.

PRINCIPLE: Being right and delivering your point incorrectly is just as bad as being wrong. You will get the same results as being wrong.

It's your choice really. You can satisfy your flesh by yelling at your husband and children; never getting your point across and never resolving the issue. It will repeat often as if you never said anything. OR, you can use your Secret Weapon and fix the problem with minimal effort.

I'm lazy, I'd rather save myself the time and effort by fixing the issue quickly so I can press on.

Before you accuse me of teaching you to treat your husband like a dog. Let me ask you this: When have you ever tired of compliments, affirmations and praise? We all thrive better with plenty of praise, compliments and affirmations.

Let's face it, it takes an adult to use their Secret Weapon and give Trophies.

8

WHAT DOES A MAN NEED?

Like you, your husband has core needs that must be met in order for your relationship to thrive. This book is written for you; rest assured that I will be covering your core needs with him in "The Husband's Toolbox".

In order to better understand the needs of a man, let's clarify the difference between needs and wants. I cover this with all my study cases so that they understand the difference. Below is a list of some needs and wants for most women, I think that you will agree with my list:

NEEDS
Air   Water
Food   Clothes

WANTS
Nice Home   Expensive Car
Pretty Dress   Classy Purse

Now that we are clear on what a need is, you can now see the basic level that these needs are derived.

NEED #1

To be honored.

A man who is belittled by his wife will increase the use of his wall to protect himself like he does when is out of the house. This can range from embarrassing him in public to ridicule when you are home. The following scripture has been used to bash women for years and this is not my intent. However, if we are going to cover this from a biblical perspective, then we must be aware of what the scriptures share.

Eph 5:33 Nevertheless let every one of you in particular so love his wife even as himself; and the wife [see] that she reverence [her] husband.

Reverence is defined in the Greek as a form of fear or respect and honor, to give preferential treatment. You actually fulfill a portion of this with your Secret Weapon.

NEED #2

To be accepted as he is.

Your husband may have a wall up a lot but he knows when you are trying to change him. There is a difference between trying to change him and drawing out of him the man you see inside. Your Secret Weapon along with the other challenges in this book help you cross over to drawing him out.

When you meet his need to be accepted as he is, he will be less defensive. This is where your secret weapon comes in handy. It will continue to reaffirm that you accept him, even when you are angry with him.

It is imperative that you do not use the "D" word (divorce) when you are arguing. It tears at the security of the marriage and he will begin to stop trusting you in other areas as well. You do not want to have to recover from this type of mistake. If you have already done so, stop and pray that God intervene on your behalf to get past it.

NEED #3

To be included in your life.

In a world where your husband faces rejection and exclusion on a daily basis, he is looking for a place where he is consistently included. Your Secret Weapon fulfills that need perfectly.

NEED #4

Sex

Yes, sex is a need. He also has a need to know that you want him sexually and that he satisfies you. This is why Challenge #2 is so important. Nothing communicates this message to him like Challenge #2.

WHAT IS THE MEANING OF SEX

Some say sex is for when all is well between you two. Nothing could be further from the truth. It is OK to have sex in the middle of a disagreement. Sex helps solidify the marriage. I encourage women to have sex with their husbands, afterwards, tell them that it was good and that you are still not OK with... Or that you have not changed your mind concerning...

This type of strategy forces the husband to deal with the issue because he cannot use the lack of sex as a barrier. Trust me when I tell you that men will use lack of sex as a reason for a lot of things.

Sex was designed by God. In His infinite wisdom, he made it so that it is pleasurable for both parties. Even at an older age. Sarah, Abraham's wife confessed this in Genesis

Ge 18:11 Now Abraham and Sarah [were] old [and] well stricken in age; [and] it ceased to be with Sarah after the manner of women. **12** Therefore Sarah laughed within herself, saying, After I am waxed old shall I have pleasure, my lord being old also?

Sarah clearly confesses that Abraham and her had sex for pleasure as well as to procreate. God brought it back into their lives to make a barren womb conceive a child. Sex is for pleasure and procreation.

Note: Doing things on this earth is very spiritual. If you elect not to steel, you are obeying a spiritual law. You are also fellowshipping with the spirit of obedience. When you are sexually active with your spouse, you are fellowshipping with the spirit of obedience. Not to mention the power of becoming one physically typifies the oneness in the spirit. Even God operates in the spiritual and natural simultaneously. The spiritual types the natural. See Romans 1:20.

Ro 1:20 For the invisible things of him from the creation of the world are clearly seen, being understood by the things that are made, [even] his eternal power and Godhead; so that they are without excuse:

WHY DOES HE NEED SEX?

Your husband married you. This is no light commitment from him. This also speaks of his desire to be with you. A man of this type of commitment is confronted with the desire to be as close as possible with you. Sex is the closest he can get on this earth. In fact, he probably can't get enough of it. Yes, there are additional benefits and it can be fun.

I would like to take a moment to ensure you are aware of the dynamics of sex; from a man's point of view. Your husband wants to be successful in everything he does to include sex. Your role is to teach him what you like; not what you don't like. When you are in the act and he is doing something that you don't prefer, tell him right there that you like it when he does xxxxx and that you want him to do that now. In his mind, he is thinking, "OK! she is really into this" and it will be very stimulating for him. Truth be told, the best sex he will ever have will be when you are getting what you need. If it feels good to you, it will most likely feel good to him. I believe God made man and woman that way physically and psychologically. So, make sure you teach him what you like. He will thank you for it.

Also know that the female body is a mystery to your husband and he will never get tired of learning how to please you. As in all things, if he thinks he can be successful, he is all in! The bible shares in 1 Peter 3: 7.

1 Peter 3:7 Likewise, **ye husbands, dwell with them according to knowledge,** giving honour unto the wife, as unto the weaker vessel, and as being heirs together of the grace of life; that your prayers be not hindered.

Let me say here that this scripture forced me into an important question: What knowledge is this scripture talking about? After prayer and learning these principles, I believe the answer is the knowledge that the wife teaches him. I am more concerned with what my wife likes than what women like. So is your husband. Teach him with your Secret Weapon and Trophies; you're going to love the results!!!

What is allowed and not allowed in the marriage bed? I get asked this often. My best advice is this; the bible says:

Heb 13:4 Marriage [is] honourable in all, and the bed undefiled: but whoremongers and adulterers God will judge.

Please try to stay with the natural use of the body. Unnatural uses of the body are contradictory to God's design and purpose. Look up Romans 1:16-27 in your bible. This should help you understand what God defines as the natural use of the body.

Just so that I know you know, here are some things you should know. There are always exceptions, however, generally these hold true for most. He and/or you may not know this so discuss it using your Secret Weapon.

- Women can have more than one orgasm. You may not need to rest to go again. You going for another will be very exciting to him.

- Men can have more than one orgasm. Just give him a minute before you start again. But you don't have to stop completely. If he's still erect, there is still potential.

- Men love to hear positive feedback during sex. This is not the time for an expresser to get quiet. He wants to succeed with you and feedback encourages him to go for the finish line; even if it is in whispers and soft moans. He will love it!!!

- Some men may fall asleep after sex. Chemically it is not unusual. According to LiveScience, an article entitled "Why do guys get sleepy after sex?"

Research shows that during ejaculation, men release a cocktail of brain chemicals, including norepinephrine, serotonin, oxytocin, vasopressin, nitric oxide (NO), and the hormone prolactin. The release of prolactin is linked to the feeling of sexual satisfaction, and it also mediates the "recovery time" that men are well aware of—the time a guy must wait before "giving it another go." Studies have also shown that men deficient in prolactin have faster recovery times.

Prolactin levels are naturally higher during sleep, and animals injected with the chemical become tired immediately. This suggests a strong link between prolactin and sleep, so it's likely that the hormone's release during orgasm causes men to feel sleepy.

Oxytocin and vasopressin, two other chemicals released during orgasm, are also associated with sleep. Their release frequently accompanies that of melatonin, the primary hormone that regulates our body clocks. Oxytocin is also thought to reduce stress levels, which again could lead to relaxation and sleepiness.
(article: http://www.livescience.com/32445-why-do-guys-get-sleepy-after-sex.html)

The art of learning is repetition. So, practice, practice, practice! ☺

As previously mentioned, Men need to know if you desire them sexually. Verbally confirming that you do is not enough evidence. You will have to get him in a headlock and take him into the bedroom yourself to seal the deal. Not all the time; just enough to keep him on his toes. Without following through with the act, your words will become meaningless and frustrating to him.

HOW MUCH IS TOO MUCH SEX

This question comes up a lot and I would like to say that fourteen times a day is ok if you both agree to it. To find the right balance for your relationship, I recommend the pendulum effect. A pendulum finds the center (or balance) by swinging to extremes.

What this means is try to have more sex than you both can possibly stand and then go for a while until someone wants some. Somewhere in the middle is your balance.

SAYING NO TO SEX

The bible shares that the only time to avoid sex is for a time of fasting and prayer; of which both of you have agreed on. Ladies, if you are led to go on a fast, use your secret weapon and tell him so and for how long. The bible says that you are to come together immediately after to keep the enemy from getting in. So, if you end your fasting and prayer early, tell him that it's time for sex.

1Corinthians 7: 2 Nevertheless, [to avoid] fornication, let every man have his own wife, and let every woman have her own husband. **3** Let the husband render unto the wife due benevolence: and likewise also the wife unto the husband. **4**

The wife hath not power of her own body, but the husband: and likewise also the husband hath not power of his own body, but the wife. 5 Defraud ye not one the other, except [it be] with consent for a time, that ye may give yourselves to fasting and prayer; and come together again, that Satan tempt you not for your incontinency.

Sometimes you are just too exhausted for sex and you are asking for mercy. So how do you tell him that you don't want to have sex when he asks? Use your secret weapon and tell him that you enjoy having sex with him but you are so tired and would love to take a raincheck. Then promise him when you can have sex. DANGER! You must keep your word. Empty promises will create impatience and anger. If something comes up that prevents you from keeping your promise, be the first one to bring it up and tell him when you can. Don't delay too many times and always be the first one to bring it up. This will let him know that you haven't forgotten him.

If he insists on sex, try your best to rock his world and make sure you get yours too. No sense in getting into it without a happy ending for all.

If you are doing Challenge #2 regularly, and letting him initiate sex as well, then rainchecks will be easily tolerated. If the interruptions are not easily tolerated, maybe it's time for you to get him in a headlock and drag him to the bedroom.

Sex is very beneficial for both the male and female. Don't discard the power of the "quickie" either. It brings you both as physically close as possible. Spiritually, it increases your bond. Emotionally, it helps you maintain some balance. Finally, biologically, it is healthy for you both.

THE ONLY WAY TO CHANGE YOUR MINDSET

For whatever reason, if you disagree with the mentality laid out above. I encourage you to ignore your reasoning and do all the suggestions; at least for a year. If you will totally commit to these principles for one year, you will discover a new you and you will like her.

NEED #5

Trophies

I know that I have covered this already. But I cannot over-emphasize the power of you showing approval of your husband. What other indication is going to help him win with you? A plain verbal "thank you" is for friends, women and strangers. He is your husband. He should be above all other humans.

When your husband does something that you like, and would like him to repeat, you need to give him a trophy. We men love trophies and will always be willing to win another one. It is trophies that teach men what it takes to win. If we are winning, then our wives are blessed and joyful.

What does a trophy consist of? Like real trophies, several parts make the whole and all parts are required to complete the trophy. A trophy from you consists of:

> A hug
> A kiss
> A look in his eyes
> Whisper to him that he did good and/or thank him

He will repeat anything that gives him a trophy and stop doing things that don't earn a trophy. It's up to you to encourage what you want from him. It is also your task to reinforce the things that you want. Give him a trophy!

9

- -

TAKE THE
CHALLENGE!

The purpose of these challenges is to tremendously increase your influence in the relationship and provoke such curiosity in your husband that he wants to know more about what he can do to bless you.

I will admit that you are going to have a blast at tormenting him in such a wonderful way, that he will try to find out what made you do these wonderfully unexpected things.

Now would be a good time to go over the rules of engagement.

1. For now, do not tell him where you are getting these ideas. If he asks, simply say "Can't a wife love on her husband?"

   Here is the fun part! When you say that to him, he is thinking that if he says no, you will stop doing what you are doing and he doesn't want that. If he says yes, then he cannot continue to ask about the sudden changes. You win!!!

2. You cannot tell him about this book until you have completed all three challenges and waited for the specified time afterward.

   You want to allow him to marinate over the last event so that you can peak his interest.

3. Try to do all three challenges as given to you with as little deviation as possible.

4. Have Fun!!!!

   Throughout the challenges, you get to watch your husband try to figure out what exactly is going on. He loves what you're doing but he can't connect the dots on how all this came about. For a man, this will cause him to do a lot of thinking about you. You will get to enjoy the struggle you see on his face... Lots of fun for you!!!!

   Incidentally, men love women with a facet of mystery in their lives. It is very appealing.

So, let's get busy!

CHALLENGE #1

The first day:

Privately sit down beside him, gently touch him and whisper the following:

"You know how you get relief for stress by thinking about it? I get the same relief from stress when I talk about it. If I keep trying to get you to talk about it, you will be interrupted from dealing with the stress. I also am interrupted when you interrupt me and try to help me fix things by making suggestions."

Next: Tell him something that you would like him to do for you with your Secret Weapon.

If he does not respond, smile, get up and press on with your daily business.

WHAT IS GOING ON WITH HIM?

At this point he is not sure what just happened. You did something different, he liked it but he can't figure out where this came from. He'll think about it for the next day or so. His first thought may be that it was a fluke and it won't happen again. We usually think that way when we can't get our heads around it. LOL. It's true.

WHAT IS IN IT FOR YOU?

You have just begun the first seed of mystery with him. Congratulations! Trust me when I tell you that this will fester; especially when you do it again the next day.

The next day use your Secret Weapon to address something important to you. He is unable to resist you and will not respond the same way he has in the past. The wall is not engaged. He will be like putty in your hands. So be merciful but honest.

Continue to use your Secret Weapon every day. Use it for funny things, emotional things, serious things, good things and bad things. This must become your normal mode of operation. Every time you use it, he will be convinced something is up! This is a good thing.

Take the time to look at him as you use your Secret Weapon, enjoy the perplexed look on his face. He is caught between loving what you are doing and experiencing you enter directly into his heart without resistance. It takes some getting used to, but he will thank you for it in the end.

CHALLENGE #2

On the third day or there about:

Tell your husband that you have something very important to discuss with him in the bedroom. Close the door, and as you speak to him in a whisper about something you want him to know, begin taking his clothes off. If he asks you what you are doing, just tell him that you need him to listen to what you are saying. Have your way with him sexually. Stay in charge and don't stop until YOU are satisfied.

Please remember, this is focused on blowing his mind by you not doing what he expects from you.

WHAT IS GOING ON WITH HIM?

He LOVES it! The moment will make him forget about everything and he might even be embarrassed. But, He will NOT want you to stop. This is a core need; you are hitting it right on the bull's-eye! DO NOT let your temperament, or the old you stop from meeting your need. If he tries to take over, tell him that it is your turn and that you got this! He will like this because he is stimulated by you being stimulated.

Note: You will have great success if you focus on what you like. The rule of engagement is: This is all about you getting yours. He will get his, no worries there. If you are not into it... Fake it! The goal is to throw him off what he expects you will do.

Have Fun!

WHAT IS IN IT FOR YOU?

He will be provoked to go out of his way to do something for you. You will draw something out of him that you didn't know existed. It will be a good thing and you will appreciate it. Not to mention that you will enjoy the challenge as well. My wife and I have found that sex is a lot like life; you get out of it what you put into it.

CHALLENGE #3

On the fifth day or there about:

Have your husband sit down somewhere where you can wash his feet. Get a towel and a pan with warm water; put a couple of drops of olive oil in the water. Kneel down and wash his feet. Take the time to message the oil into his feet. While doing so, tell him how much you love him and appreciate him for who he is and what he does for you. Be specific and general in your appreciation. When you have dried his feet, tell him "**You Are My King**". Do not misquote this.

If you have to persuade him, use your Secret Weapon. Tell him that you need to. If he insists, tell him that it would hurt your feelings if he denies you.

Don't be afraid to kneel at his feet, you are not enabling him to be more domineering. This has a dramatically different effect on men than you may think.

Jesus washed his disciples' feet, he then asked them to wash others feet.

WHAT IS GOING ON WITH HIM?

He will most likely be overwhelmed, embarrassed or even blush. To a man, this is one of the greatest honors you can bestow on him. He will most likely feel awkward and extremely vulnerable. This will catch him totally off guard and if he stutters, just know that you've got him right where you want him.

WHAT IS IN IT FOR YOU?

When you said to him "You Are My King", he now has an idea of how highly you hold him. As a man, I can tell you that he will do everything in his power to stay there! It is one thing to earn that place of honor and another if it is given to a man to maintain. He will kill himself to stay there. Really! Consequently, you win!!!

You are actually showing him how you would handle his heart by handling his feet. This will cause him to trust that he can open up to you without condemnation or ridicule. He may even decide to wash yours at some point. Regardless of the past, this will pull out of him more of the man that you saw when you married him. It doesn't even matter if you have been married for a short or long time. It doesn't matter if you and your husband are of great prestige. These challenges will revolutionize your marriage.

Now it is time to Tell Him!

Pray this first:

Lord Jesus, move on my husband when I tell him about the book I want him to read; The Husband's Toolbox. And let him read this book and put to practice what he has learned. In Jesus Name, Amen

Now you may tell him where you got these ideas from. Ask him if he liked them and if they made the relationship better. Also tell him that you have a book for him to read that was written by the same author (The Husbands Toolbox). He will be most willing to read this book after his experience with you over the past week or so.

CHALLENGE #4

Retrain yourself to gently touch him and whisper when you are angry or emotional. This will have a dramatic effect on him. He will get it and respond much better than if you put a voice to your anger. Repeat the first three challenges on a regular basis at first and then maybe once a quarter. He will never get tired of them and you will never get tired of the results from him.

WHAT IS GOING ON WITH HIM?

He will like the fact that you are keeping him informed and will try to correct things if he is the source of your anger. You are more than likely not going to have to cover that subject again.

WHAT IS IN IT FOR YOU?

You will have more peace and pleasure in your house and it will be less effort for you to correct issues as they arise. Now you two can mature together and truly become one.

FINALLY

Make these challenges a regular staple in your relationship. They are guaranteed to increase and maintain the two of you together.

I wish you all the success in the world... I wish you Jesus!

10

- -

YOUR ROLE

FROM A BIBLICAL PERSPECTIVE

Many times, the bible is used to force women to comply. This is not my intent here. Rather it is my desire to use these scriptures to show you how influential you are when you operate in your God given nature as a nester, nurturer and relational being.

1Pe 5:5 ¶ Likewise, ye younger, submit yourselves unto the elder. Yea, all [of you] **be subject one to another**, and be clothed with humility: for God resisteth the proud, and giveth grace to the humble.

The scripture above clearly delineates that Husbands and Wives should be subject to each other. This means that even though God has placed the man as the head of the family, he must be subject to his wife.

The Greek word for Subject is **υποτασσω** hupotasso (pronounced hoop-ot-as'-so) meaning to submit one's self. It implies that the husband and wife must place themselves in submission to each other. Notice that it does not say that they should make the other submit. Basically, you are required to place yourself under submission.

It also means:

> to submit to one's control

> to yield to one's admonition or advice

> to obey, be subject

1 Peter 3:1 ¶ Likewise, ye wives, be in subjection to your own husbands; that, if any obey not the word, they also may without the word be won by the conversation of the wives; **2** While they behold your chaste conversation coupled with fear. **3** Whose adorning let it not be that outward adorning of plaiting the hair, and of wearing of gold, or of putting on of apparel; **4** But let it be the hidden man of the heart, in that which is not corruptible, even the ornament of a meek and quiet spirit, which is in the sight of God of great price. **5** For after this manner in the old time the holy women also, who trusted in God, adorned themselves, being in subjection unto their own husbands: **6** Even as Sara obeyed Abraham, calling him lord: whose daughters ye are, as long as ye do well, and are not afraid with any amazement. **7** Likewise, ye husbands, dwell with them according to knowledge, giving honour unto the wife, as unto the weaker vessel, and as being heirs together of the grace of life; that your prayers be not hindered.

Verse 4 through 6 is emphasizing the importance for women to concentrate on keeping a pure heart and that adorning or wearing gold and silver is second to the heart. It is not telling women to avoid wearing gold and silver.

Verse 7 does not claim that women are weaker; it directs men to give honor to the wife AS the weaker vessel. It also instructs the men that when they do this their prayers won't be hindered.

Nowhere in the bible will you find it saying that women are second class citizens. You will find women who knew their God given persuasiveness and used it for a Godly outcome. This is what I am hoping you will receive here; the knowledge of your persuasive powers and how to use them for a Godly outcome.

Col 3:19 Husbands, love [your] wives, and be not bitter against them.

Eph 5:25 Husbands, love your wives, even as Christ also loved the church, and gave himself for it;

There are many more references but I think that these clearly identify the role of the Husband and the role of the Wife from a biblical perspective.

I would like to emphasize that marriage God's way provides a 100% chance of success.

All spouses feel unappreciated at times. Jesus was unappreciated and rejected for us as well. So serve him and don't expect to be served all the time. Jesus, The Son Of God, served people, washed their feet, prayed for them, and encouraged them. You must do the same. The more you focus on being unappreciated, the more you will be miserable. When your priorities are right, your joy will be right.

Pastor Philip Campbell put it best!

> J O Y
>
> J = Jesus First
>
> O = Others Next (Family)
>
> Y = Yourself last
>
> Selfish people are never happy and never have joy.

As a wife, pray for your husband. Ask God to guide him towards the things of God. This is a loaded prayer as God desires for you and him to be happy in your marriage.

11

MARRIAGE
DYNAMICS

There are many dynamics in a marriage that go unaddressed before, during or after a marriage. It is my desire to cover a few of them in this chapter. I used to hear people say that marriage is hard work but I never really understood that. Now I have come to know that there are dynamics in my marriage that I strive to improve on so that my wife and I can enjoy our marriage. I will never tell you that we have perfected everything, however I will tell you that we are constantly apologizing and trying again; whatever the dynamic that we are working on. I will never tell you that this is easy but I will tell you that it is rewarding.

It is best to look at this as a work in progress for the rest of your life. Granted, the art of learning is repetition, and through constant use, you will be very successful. However, you must never allow yourself to be satisfied with what you have achieved. It is imperative that you continue to perfect your skills; regardless of the success.

MARRIAGE IS AN ENTITY ALL OF ITS OWN

There are four entities in a marriage:

God, Marriage, The Man, and The Woman

According to God, marriage is not an action or a fad. It is a binding covenant between a man and a woman. With God, all covenants are living testaments to something greater than the two who entered into it. When God entered into a covenant with Abraham, He kept his word. When God told Abraham that he would be the father of many nations, God entered into a covenant with Abraham and it became so. All throughout the bible, covenants were taken very seriously by God and man. Today, covenants are just as weighty as they were then. There are powerful forces at work when we enter into a covenant. My prayer is that you realize the power behind your covenant of marriage.

If we treat marriage like a living entity, then we will make decisions and govern ourselves for the sake of the marriage and Jesus Christ; even when we lack interest.

Remember that your priority is God first, your spouse, then children, yourself, and finally your extended family and friends. Any time this order is changed, your walk will become a lot harder. Also, your children are learning from you how to prioritize family. It is healthy for them to see you make their father more important; there is a sense of security they derive from this.

11.1

Trust Is Earned!

Trust is earned, not given away freely. I had a car salesman, of whom I have never met, ask me "don't you trust me?". I replied with the above sentence.

Trust is also multilevel. My trust with a car salesman requires minimal verification compared to a relationship with someone I call my friend. Even more is required for my spouse. It was former president Ronald Reagan who said "Trust but verify!" Verification is vital to deep trust. Like an onion, the more your spouse trusts you, the more they will reveal their heart to you. I remember one incident where my wife told me something about herself that took ten years of marriage to earn her trust.

So, it's our responsibility to confirm our loyalty to our spouse anytime they ask us where we've been, who we're speaking with on the phone, texting, reading, or looking at on the computer/TV. The more they ask, the more opportunity we have to earn more trust. This is especially important if there have been some incidences that have created mistrust.

WARNING! Any defensive response or sign of impatience with the questions will most likely be interpreted as guilt of wrong doing.

If you have lost your spouse's trust, you can earn it back but it will take some time and humility on your part. The more trust that you have lost, the more time and humility it will require.

If you are now asking "How long do I have to endure the questions?" It may be time to see a pastor who can help you and your spouse address any issues peculiar to your situation. I recommend a Christian counselor you trust...

I can recommend Pastor Anthony McMillan, Founder and CEO of HD Relationships. He is also the Senior Pastor of Life Church, Pensacola, Florida. His given gift from God is helping relationships reach a level of High Definition. Take time to look them up on Facebook or online at www.plife.org You'll be glad that you did!

11.2

Dictionaries
HIS & HERS & THEIRS

Early in my marriage, my wife and I would go out on a date as we still do. But back then, once we got home, I would say "Honey I had a Fantastic Time!" She would reply "It was Alright." My ego would take a major hit. Many date nights were ruined by the ensuing arguments because I thought she was saying that she didn't enjoy herself when I witnessed her smiles and laughter. Not to mention my pride was hurt because I thought I did good.

Finally, God made it painfully clear that maybe she was saying something different than what I thought. After another date night, I said the same thing and she replied the same way. But this time, I stopped and said "Babe, when I was growing up, alright meant that I was just getting by. Is that what you mean?" To my surprise, she said "No, alright was like saying awesome."

Right then I realized that all this time we were in, what I like to call, violent agreement. We were saying the same thing with different words.

Now when she says "alright" I think: That's right! I'm the Man!!!

This is where the dictionary principle comes in.

When you were a child, for survival reasons, you adopted your parent's terms and definitions. You had no choice because it was the only game in town for you to learn how to communicate. No getting around this one.

However, over time, you have become so comfortable with your dictionary of terms that you are tempted to assume that everyone around you has the same dictionary. Nothing could be further from the truth.

When two people from two different families get married, there is an inevitable collision of terms about to take place. How does one protect themselves from this type of conflict? It is very easy.

Remember to ask what the other person means before you assume that they mean your negative definition. Take the time to explain to them what it means to you. Then ask them for their definition.

You have just begun creating a third dictionary. This dictionary is unique because it connects two different words to one meaning.

Sometimes, my wife will say fantastic for me. This carries a double blessing: she had a great time and she wanted to use my word to put a little extra with it…. Nice huh?

If you fail to stay calm and investigate the meaning. You will not move forward in understanding each other and the subject at hand will come up again. Don't be as slow as I was; get it right as soon as possible. It will save you a huge amount of time and effort. Trust me on this one!

11.3

I Need.... I Need

For years, I would tell my wife that I needed something from her and she would go right in to telling me what she needed from me. This used to frustrate me because I would end up feeling like she was retorting back an unmet need that I have yet to provide. It would make me feel that we are at a stalemate; until you meet my needs, I won't meet yours. I would end up thinking; I am going to stop telling her my needs because she just keeps firing back at me.

Finally, one day, I explained to her how I felt when she did that and that is when I got a new revelation.

She wasn't discounting my need; she was getting into the mode of sharing needs. This is how she put it: She said "When I talk to my sisters, someone would say that they need to get a new blouse. Then another would say that they need to get a couch for the family room and another would say that they need to get their car cleaned." My wife thought I was going into a sharing needs conversation so she chimed in.

You may be sharing a need with your spouse and they may respond by sharing a need of theirs. It may be that they are not retorting with their unmet need. The underlying issue here may be: you could have taken care of that need and did not; this could make you a little defensive.

HOW TO ADDRESS YOUR SPOUSE'S NEEDS

When your spouse starts off the need sharing conversation, address that need before you share your need. It even helps to ask them if they would like to hear ONE of your needs since we are on the subject. If the answer is no, then you should respond with "OK, maybe another time."

When I bring up one of my needs to my wife, I want her to respond to my need first. This makes me feel like she is listening and cares about my needs. Once she addresses my need, she can share her need. Try to keep it to one need at a time. If one person names off many needs, then the one listening may feel that they don't have a right to their need. That is unfair! Don't be that gal!

No matter how small the need, if your spouse mentions a need to you, you are responsible for treating that need with care. Celebrating your differences includes allowing each to share their needs; regardless of how great or small.

My wife places the knives in the silverware holder blade down because I told her that I didn't want anyone to get hurt reaching for a fork. This is one of my needs.

I try to help my wife with her projects around the house because that is one of her needs.

11.4

Customer Service

Not all customer service centers are open 24/7. However, if you want your husband's customer service center to stay open more often, you will need to keep your customer service center open as much as possible. If you are the first to open your customer service center for more hours, trust me when I tell you that it will pay big dividends!!!

It will also help if you use your secret weapon. Spouses are not ready at a moment's notice to listen to what you have to say 24/7. Wives, remember that men are not verbally stimulated as women.

So, when you want to talk, a gentle touch and whisper will cause him to be more tuned to what you have to say and he will want to listen. Then you will find that he can respond to you like a real human being.

Men and boys are physically and visually stimulated. When you touch them, it alerts them to be able to hear what you have to say. Additionally, men/boys love to be touched by their wives/moms. It meets a core need because it tells them that they are accepted and it draws them to want more touches; thus, a willing heart to listen.

Your secret weapon will stimulate a willingness to listen and comply, it will alleviate a lot of stress on your part. This process will work with men and your sons.

Please don't forget that you are also obligated to provide good customer service as well. The more you touch your husband, the more you will meet a core need that he has. The more you whisper to your husband, the more you will make him feel that he is included in your life; this is a bigger issue than you may think. Whispering meets another core need and it will provoke him to want to please you.

Your job is to keep your customer service window open as much as possible. This means you may want to be more empathetic to your spouse's needs. Doing the challenges teaches you the core needs of your man and how to meet them. The better you become at meeting them, the more influential you become to him. It's really a win-win situation.

Some men resent their wives withholding sex because of stress, arguments and for what other reasons. Ladies, having sex only when you are in agreement is a fallacy. It's OK for you to have sex with your husband and then afterward let him know that you are still not happy about the situation. This will speak louder to him than you can imagine. You are more likely to get faster results if you do.

Remember that customer service representatives try to meet their customer's needs and sometimes don't always agree with the customer. If this can be done in business, how much more should you do that to the one who committed to marry you. In plain English, you don't have to be in perfect agreement or feel in love to use your secret weapon or have sex. You see, if you only give him a gentle touch and sex when you like the situation, you are engaged in an exchange of services; some people call that prostitution.

11.5

Don't Assume You Know!

Women have an intuition that most men do not have. In fact, they tend to rely on it heavily. If you ever find yourself thinking "he did this because ...". You are assuming that you know why he did something without asking him. It becomes a problem when you are so convinced that you know what your husband means that you don't bother to ask him. This type of mindset will foster negative reinforcement about your husband and it will cloud your judgement of what really is coming from his heart. So, ask before you jump to conclusions.

Seeing the truth is harder when you have been hurt in the past from your childhood, other relationships and/or your husband. It's easy to be defensive once you have been hurt; too easy. One of the ways to heal and create a new mindset with your husband is to ask him what he meant by ..... Then it is your responsibility to take him at his word. In other words, you can't trust your beliefs; you must accept and adopt his explanation.

Early in our marriage, my wife would assume I meant one thing when I meant another. She wouldn't ask me what I meant and it would pile up and fester. I felt like I was being framed, tried, judged and sentenced without being allowed to have a defense. That is a helpless feeling.

My wife thought that I was blaming her for things when that was the furthest thing from my mind. Once she started asking me if I was blaming her, I was able to affirm that I wasn't. Over time, she began to know that my heart was not about blaming her. All because she kept asking until it wasn't a question.

My point here is, do not nail a meaning or motive on your husband until he has been given ample room to verbally try to convey his meaning. Please remember that you are asking a non-expresser to clarify by expressing it. That is why I said ample room. To clarify further, if you have repeated what he said over and over until he has not made any additions or continued to clarify, then he has been given ample room.

I ask that you leave room for him to clarify a misunderstanding or situation. No man wants to purposely anger his wife. If you continue to assign meanings and motives on him without giving him a say, you will cause him to stone wall you and he will not trust you with his heart. However, if you continue to allow him to clarify what he means, he will appreciate the respect you are showing him.

11.6

Influencing Decisions

The 25th chapter 1st Samuel shares a story of Nabal who refused to give David and his men provisions for the protection that they had provided. David was so angry that he prepared his men to destroy all the men in Nabal's charge. Abigail, Nabal's wife, heard of the situation and quickly loaded up provisions and met David and his men on their way to destroy Nabal.

1Sa 25:20 And it was [so, as] she rode on the ass, that she came down by the covert of the hill, and, behold, David and his men came down against her; and she met them.

1Sa 25:23 And when Abigail saw David, she hasted, and lighted off the ass, and fell before David on her face, and bowed herself to the ground, **24** And fell at his feet, and said, Upon me, my lord, [upon] me [let this] iniquity [be]: and let thine handmaid, I pray thee, speak in thine audience, and hear the words of thine handmaid.

1Sa 25:27 And now this blessing which thine handmaid hath brought unto my lord, let it even be given unto the young men that follow my lord. **28** I pray thee, forgive the trespass of thine handmaid: for the LORD will certainly make my lord a sure house; because my lord fighteth the battles of the LORD, and evil hath not been found in thee [all] thy days.

1Sa 25:30 And it shall come to pass, when the LORD shall have done to my lord according to all the good that he hath spoken concerning thee, and shall have appointed thee ruler over Israel; **31** That this shall be no grief unto thee, nor offence of heart unto my lord, either that thou hast shed blood causeless, or that my lord hath avenged himself: but when the LORD shall have dealt well with my lord, then remember thine handmaid.

David then answers this woman who honored him for who he is and who he will become:

1Sa 25:33 And blessed [be] thy advice, and blessed [be] thou, which hast kept me this day from coming to [shed] blood, and from avenging myself with mine own hand. **34** For in very deed, [as] the LORD God of Israel liveth, which hath kept me back from hurting thee, except thou hadst hasted and come to meet me, surely there had not been left unto Nabal by the morning light any that pisseth against the wall. **35** So David received of her hand [that] which she had brought him, and said unto her, Go up in peace to thine house; see, I have hearkened to thy voice, and have accepted thy person.

Nabal dies the next morning because God judged his wrong doing. Then David sends for Abagail to be his wife.

1Sa 25:39 And when David heard that Nabal was dead, he said, Blessed [be] the LORD, that hath pleaded the cause of my reproach from the hand of Nabal, and hath kept his servant from evil: for the LORD hath returned the wickedness of Nabal upon his own head. And David sent and communed with Abigail, to take her to him to wife. **40** And when the servants of David were come to Abigail to

Carmel, they spake unto her, saying, David sent us unto thee, to take thee to him to wife. **41** And she arose, and bowed herself on [her] face to the earth, and said, Behold, [let] thine handmaid [be] a servant to wash the feet of the servants of my lord. **42** And Abigail hasted, and arose, and rode upon an ass, with five damsels of hers that went after her; and she went after the messengers of David, and became his wife.

Abigail wasn't acting like this because women were of lesser value then. She knew the power of influence she had in honoring David. I'm sure she practiced this same technique with Nabal. How do you think Nabal was so prosperous? Folly (the meaning of Nabal) can never prosper. It had to be from Abigail's influence that made Nabal make prosperous decisions.

YOU MUST LET THEM MAKE THEIR OWN MISTAKES

While trying to influence your husband's decision, remember that you will not be able to influence all of his decisions. Partly because God will use that to teach you some things and part will be he has to make his own mistakes to learn just as you do.

Your disposition in these times should be patient, caring loving and accepting. Remember Proverbs 21:1.

Pr 21:1 ¶ The king's heart [is] in the hand of the LORD, [as] the rivers of water: he turneth it whithersoever he will.

This scripture not only speaks of one who rules a nation or a kingdom, it also speaks of authority over us. Did you notice that it didn't say that the authority over you had to be saved? It simply said that God will turn him as God wills. Your prayers should focus on pleasing God so that God will turn your husband to be a blessing for you in spite of himself.

When discussing a decision that needs to be made with your husband, don't allow yourself to answer with "Just do whatever you want because you are going to do it anyway." This is very provocative and it undermines the fact that he was discussing it with you before making the decision. Understand your husband, maybe he needs to talk about all the possibilities (even the bad ones) before he can see the situation clearly. This is the time for you to listen and help him come up with the best ideas for him to choose from. Below are some ideas of what to say and not to say.

DO SAY:

> Have you thought about...
>
> I like this idea...
>
> I think this might be the best idea, what do you think?
>
> I really don't have a preference.
>
> I know that you will make the right decision for the family.
>
> Thank you for talking with me before you made the decision; I can see that you are trying to make this a joint effort. (if you give him a trophy with this, you will see him do it more)
>
> With all that we have discussed, I want you to do what God would have you do. (This puts an incredible amount of weight on him to be sure God is pleased; even if he is unsaved)

DON'T SAY

> Just do whatever you want because you are going to do it anyway.

> I don't care!

> It doesn't matter what I think!

> Who cares?

> You never listen to me anyway.

The things you should say will help you create an atmosphere of trust and he will learn that he can approach you with more decisions. It is sort of him testing you to see if he can trust you with his heart. If he can engage in basic decision making process with you, then maybe he can engage in more difficult decisions with you. The more difficult the decisions he can talk to you about, the more you will hear his heart and how he feels about many things.

WHEN THINGS GO WRONG

It's not a matter of if, but when things go wrong. The human race cannot be flawless. So, let's talk about how you should respond to these situations.

First, realize if anything can be done to reverse the situation. Ask him this. If yes, ask him if he is going to do it (don't assume anything). If he says no, then tell him that he must have a good reason and ask him to share it with you (This type of approach gives him the benefit of the doubt). If you don't agree with his reasoning, go to the second step.

Second, ask him if he has any ideas of what should be done. After his response, if it isn't clear, ask him what you can do to help.

Third, if you have some ideas, now is a time to ask him if he is willing hear some of your ideas at this time. If he responds to not now, then revisit it with him later. Trust me when I tell you that no man wants to make a mistake, especially when it concerns his family and future; he may be a little overwhelmed at the moment.

I know that you may feel like you are taking a back seat to the relationship when you follow these steps, however, my goal is to teach you how to steer from the trunk of the car. You are designed to be influential in the relationship, you just can't get caught up with the seat you find yourself in. Besides, this type of approach is a mature way to deal with your spouse, family, and friends. For the most part, you are giving your spouse the room to make the right decision without adding undue pressure or confusion. I have found that 99.999% of people want to do the right thing and will if given the tools, support and space to do so.

MAKE A PLAN

Prayerfully create a plan together for your family, spiritually, financially and socially. Ask him what he thinks about your ideas. It's important to tell him if you are undecided so he knows what level of the process needs more discussion.

Here is a prayer you and your husband may want to say before you start:

> Lord Jesus forgive us of our sins, known and unknown, according to your word. Give us wisdom to

make decisions that would fulfill your will for us. In Jesus' Name we pray, Amen.

I used to work for an engineering firm that often went from concept to reality. The best way to accomplish this is to have all the ideas tabled; good and bad. You would be amazed at what ideas come up if the environment allows for all ideas.

Once the ideas are written down, everyone contributes to how to accomplish each idea. Once all the ideas have been entertained, everyone votes on the best idea that can be supported most efficiently. Try this with the goals you have set with your husband. Also, like my past job, revisit your goals and decision regularly to ensure that they are still lining up. If not, you may need to ask if the goal should be changed or the decision. Again, these questions are for you and your husband to decide.

Using your goals as a guide, engage in a conversation with him. Sometime during the conversation, ask him what he thinks about the goals and the decision that you both have made. Then ask him how does he feel about them. (you may be differentiating between thought and feelings for the first time so don't harp on this)

Tell him that you are glad that you both are making decisions together and be sure to give him a trophy. This will encourage to continue to keep this process in place. Don't under estimate the power that this produces between you both.

If you guys find yourself in disagreement, I encourage you to pray and take this as a sign of bad timing. Many good ideas at the wrong time can be disastrous.

Don't let this process be the catalyst for arguments. Stay calm, allowing everyone to be honest will bring the best results. The trick is to not allow yourself to get too emotionally connected to one decision. Remember that God can bring you both into agreement. Spend your time looking for agreement. Pray about the rest. Below is another technique that my wife and I use on occasion to ensure that we are making the right decision at the right time.

ANOTHER DECISION PROCESS

My wife and I use a particular scripture to make decisions when we aren't in agreement or don't know what God wants us to do.

We pray:

> "Lord Jesus forgive us of our sins, known and unknown, according to your word. Put us at one mind and accord with your spirit."
>
> "Lord, would you have us to XXXXXX?
>
> --- we listen for an answer ---
>
> Let's say one of us heard a Yes and we agree to use that answer. Then we pray:
>
> "Spirit that would have us XXXXXX, do you confess that Jesus Christ was come in the flesh?"
>
> --- if we both hear a yes, we know it's from God. ---
>
> --- if we hear no, nothing or an answer that interrupts our question, we know it's not from God. ---

---if we get a yes and a no, then it may not be the right time to do that, so we revisit it at another time. ---

This process comes from 1John 4:1-3.

1Jo 4:1 ¶ Beloved, believe not every spirit, but try the spirits whether they are of God: because many false prophets are gone out into the world. **2** Hereby know ye the Spirit of God: **Every spirit that confesseth that Jesus Christ is come in the flesh is of God: 3** And **every spirit that confesseth not that Jesus Christ is come in the flesh is not of God:** and this is that spirit of antichrist, whereof ye have heard that it should come; and even now already is it in the world.

Make no mistake about it. All of God's angels will politely wait for you to finish asking before they will answer. They are also bold to confess that Jesus Christ came in the flesh without hesitation. All other responses are not from God.

11.7

Give What You're Given

My wife's birthday was coming up and I asked my daughter and son what we should get her. My son (6 yrs.) immediately said "Let's get her a train set!" I learned an important principle here. We often give others what we want. Even as adults, we don't always investigate what someone else would like.

It is normal for two people in a marriage to have different needs. Finding out what your mate's needs are can be difficult. However, paying attention to your husband, you can learn how to meet his needs.

We humans have a habit giving to others what we desire to receive. If your husband gives you a lot of kisses, then he would love it if you would give him a lot of kisses. In fact, the more one receives what they need, the less they give what they like to receive. This is an excellent indicator on when they really have a need. If you notice that he has been touching you more often, then you can start touching him and you will meet his need.

Let me give you an example: I'm a touchy/feely person. My wife is not. I've noticed that when I want to be touched by her, I start touching her more often. This is such a subconscious act that I don't realize that I'm doing it at first. However, when she touches me, I drink it in like a cool refreshing drink after working hard outside in the sun. I just love it when she touches me; I can't get enough! I love it when she takes my hand, puts her arm in my arm, pats me on the rear, plays with my hair, etc...

Take the time to observe what your husband is giving you and try to give it back. If it is pleasant, good, caring and does not contradict the Word of God, it will be a good thing to return.

Some observations you may make are:

Does he do little things for you?

Is he a romantic type?

Does he touch you a lot?

Does he cook for you?

Does he listen to you?

Does he talk to you?

Does he give good massages?

These are some examples of what you can observe and then do them for him. Take the time to write a list of observations and then try them on him. Don't cross off anything until you ask him how he liked what you did. His nonverbal response won't always agree with how he liked something.

On the flip side, observe what you have a natural desire to do for your spouse and determine if that is what you want done to you. If so, now you can convey that to him with your secret weapon.

11.8

Artificial Intuition (AI)

Women are naturally intuitive. It is one of the gifts taken from Adam that God gave a majority to Eve. It is the reason that wives are the best judge of women when it comes to their spouse. Ladies, you must use your secret weapon when you inform him that you suspect a woman could be trouble.

With that said, men are not as intuitive. If you think that they should know something because everyone knows it, he probably doesn't. Before you get angry with him for not jumping in and helping or understanding something, ask yourself if you are expecting him to act like a woman and intuitively lock on. I would venture to say that 89% of men are not as intuitive.

Just tell him what you would like him to do! If you are doing the challenges, he will be sitting on the edge of his seat with desire to reciprocate what you have done for him. He will most likely do it for you without any push back. If you continue to ask him to do the same thing for you with a gentle touch and whisper, you will train him to do those things automatically without your need to mention it.

Soon he will be doing things that would give you the impression that he has achieved a sense of Artificial Intuitiveness. Please remember that the level at which you apply your secret weapon is the level of results you will see.

Don't forget to be patient. If you want him to do it because he wants to, then use your secret weapon.

I know that from a woman's perspective that this may seem manipulative. However, I am a man and I'm trying to tell you what moves a man. If you use these principles with a manipulative heart, remember that God will address this with you. Conversely, you should be using these techniques to create a better unity between you two and to help the relationship blossom into a beautiful flower.

Finally, remember that the key word here is ARTIFICIAL! If he falters, your secret weapon will be most effective getting him back on track; a chuckle, gentle touch, and whisper will move mountains for you.

11.9

Changing Channels

This section reminds me of two types of changes: Conversations and Maturity. For some reason this makes sense to me so please indulge me on this one.

CONVERSATION

I can be in the middle of a conversation with my wife and out of nowhere; she starts on a different subject. This is not a bad thing; it's just a woman thing. I spent some time observing my wife with her sisters and they go a mile a minute while changing subjects and all of them are in lock step. No one misses a beat. It's incredible to watch. I marvel at the speed and perception at which they communicate. If I could harness that ability I would be the greatest man alive!

Normally, if my wife changes channel on me, I try to listen a little longer to see if I can get back on track. However, my wife is patient with me when I ask "Did we change channels?" She graciously catches me up and then we are off and running again.

Changing channels happens to both of you. Sometimes your husband changes channels while talking to you. You will need to verify with him if you are on the same channel. Remember, you don't think like a man so it can happen at a moment's notice.

This is a good time to welcome yourself into the human race. We all get frustrated when we run into confusing situations. Our goal is to not allow it to take our peace.

AS WE MATURE

After being married since 1984, I've noticed that my wife and I have changed. We both have different priorities than when we were younger. Our favorite foods have changed. And many other things have changed.

This is where communication is vital for both of you. What you liked earlier in the marriage may have changed; including sex. Talk with your spouse and make the effort to honor each other's changes. This is a good time to use your secret weapon.

The only consistent thing you can count on is CHANGE. Don't be thrown off by it; expect it; embrace it. Changing channels can be very rewarding and fun.

11.10

Types of Authority

There are three types of authority that you should be aware of: Civil Authority, Domestic Authority and Spiritual Authority. These are distinct and separate. Many times, we are tempted to blend them and that can cause some frustration.

CIVIL AUTHORITY

Policemen, Judges, and civic law operate under this type of authority. Their jurisdiction is defined by the law. If we disobey the law, we can be held accountable by the enforcers of the law. It is no surprise to see a female police woman or judge who enforces the law. They are operating within their jurisdiction and it is a good thing. They are performing a leadership role. If I am pulled over by a female police officer or in the courtroom with a female judge, I have no problem submitting to their authority.

DOMESTIC AUTHORITY

In a family of one man, one woman and children; God places the responsibility of the family on the man. God holds the man responsible for leading the family in a Godly manor. He is the point of contact as far as God is concerned. Like the other authorities, someone has to be placed in the leadership role. It is the nature of things that all those who are not placed in the position of authority are expected to submit. I know that this may be sensitive subject ladies, however, God has not changed his mind on the issue.

SPIRITUAL AUTHORITY

Spiritually, the bible relays that there is neither man nor woman in heaven. It is no surprise to see male and female spiritual leaders; to include male and female apostles, prophets, evangelists, pastors and teachers. It is possible for a male pastor to be the spiritual leader of his church and get a ticket for speeding from a female police officer.

These authorities have different jurisdictions. This is why a female pastor can be the spiritual leader of her church and come under submission to her husband when she is home.

All spiritual leaders must show a lifestyle pleasing to the Lord in all jurisdictions they find themselves in. Additionally, they must be aware of their jurisdiction.

Ladies, this book was written for you. I promise that "The Husbands Toolbox" deals with the men as well.

11.11

Menopause

Much has been written about menopause. Ladies, be aware that your husband's sexual needs may continue beyond menopause. I encourage you to seek medical advice on how to meet that need if necessary.

I am reminded of Sarah who was well stricken in years when God promised Abram a son in his old age. Sarah said "shall I have pleasure?"

Ge 18:1 ¶ And the LORD appeared unto Abraham in the plains of Mamre: and he sat in the tent door in the heat of the day; **2** And he lift up his eyes and looked, and, lo, three men stood by him: and when he saw [them], he ran to meet them from the tent door, and bowed himself toward the ground, **3** And said, My Lord, if now I have found favour in thy sight, pass not away, I pray thee, from thy servant: **4** Let a little water, I pray you, be fetched, and wash your feet, and rest yourselves under the tree: **5** And I will fetch a morsel of bread, and comfort ye your hearts; after that ye shall pass on: for therefore are ye come to your servant. And they said, So do, as thou hast said. **6** And Abraham hastened into the tent unto Sarah, and said, Make ready quickly three measures of fine meal, knead [it], and make cakes upon the hearth. **7** And Abraham ran unto the herd, and fetcht a calf tender and good, and gave [it] unto a young man; and he hasted to dress it. **8** And he took butter, and milk, and the calf which he had dressed, and set [it] before them; and he stood by them under the tree, and they did eat. **9** ¶ And they said unto him, Where [is] Sarah thy wife? And he said, Behold, in the tent. **10** And he said, I will certainly return unto thee according to the time of life; and, lo, Sarah thy wife shall have a son. And Sarah heard [it] in the tent door, which [was] behind him. **11** Now Abraham and Sarah [were] old [and] well stricken in age; [and] it ceased to be with Sarah after the manner of women. **12** Therefore Sarah laughed within herself, saying, After I am waxed old shall I have pleasure, my lord being old also?

Notice that the relationship with God transcended past their age limitation? Let your relationship with Jesus transcend any obstacles you may have. God works in and through us on this three-dimensional world both spiritually and naturally. Now Sarah was restored by God for her to have pleasure. He can do the same for you.

The purpose of this section is to help you mitigate the obstacles introduced when menopause arrives. For some women, menopause causes the uterus to produce less lubricant during sex; this can be the reason for more discomfort or pain while having sex.

I encourage you to speak with your doctor about sex being less enjoyable or even painful. They will be able to give you the best advice for your particular situation.

Some conversations with our doctor and friends of similar age have mentioned the following:

> One of our doctors have said that more sex helps reduce the discomfort.

A friend mentioned olive oil for her and her husband has helped significantly.

The internet has revealed several natural products that have very positive reviews.

Ladies, men do not have a problem with you trying to figure out what works best for you to enjoy sex. Just as long as he is included in the effort. Let him know what is happening and tell him that you want to try some things to help you enjoy it more. I encourage you both to help each other. Most of all, have fun.

11.12

Timing is Everything!

Even in ministry, a couple can be so busy that they cannot spend the time required to talk about important issues. This is very dangerous as it creates a lot of collateral damage.

My wife and I are very busy in the morning getting ready for work or church. If we have not had enough time to discuss important issues throughout the week, it will begin to surface while trying to get ready in the morning. This is a recipe for a bad morning. Our comments are quick and rushed and there is no guarantee that I (a non-verbally stimulated man) will say what I really mean. This will lead to misunderstanding and offense. Additionally, it will take more time of the morning to clear up and possibly cause one or both of us to be late. For us, the mornings are not a good time for us to discuss serious issues.

Find out a good time to talk about serious and lengthy matters that allows you both to have time to respond thoughtfully and unrushed.

My pastor takes every Monday off to dedicate it to his family. I love that he does that. It reminds us all that Christianity must include success in the family. My real point here is that you must set aside some time with your spouse alone to talk about small things, middle things and big things.

We men are sometimes afraid to talk because we don't want to say anything to offend our spouse or cause a division. Our defensiveness will cause us to either say nothing or speak harshly. This is where the challenges and your secret weapon help him become less defensive.

Please remember that you have him at a verbal disadvantage (even if he is a good speaker). If the art of learning is repetition, think of it like this. You grew up speaking conversations with dolls and role playing. Most men grew up making noises for planes, trains and automobiles.

11.13

Boundaries; Your Protection!

Where ever you go in life, opportunities to take things to extreme are always available. Boundaries are a way to prepare and protect yourself from unexpected surprises that would normally catch you off guard.

Because we are talking in reference to relationships, I want to focus on some good ground rules that help you set up great boundaries to protect you from yourself, the world and the enemy.

1. Don't allow yourself to think that you can handle it without boundaries; pride comes before a fall.

    Pr 16:18 ¶ Pride [goeth] before destruction, and an haughty spirit before a fall.

2. Never do/say anything with/to the opposite sex that you would not do/say in front of your spouse. (If you are not married, then consider Jesus as your spouse.)
3. Put yourself in your spouse's place. How would you want your spouse to honor the relationship?
4. Share your boundaries with your spouse. Create an open forum to allow for modifications to be made so that both parties are respecting each other to the level required. DO NOT fall prey to the mindset "Common sense would tell you that...". Assume nothing and

don't expect the other person to be a mind reader on your expectations.

5. Pornography must be avoided at all costs! Some say you can look but you cannot touch. Jesus says:

Mt 5:27 ¶ Ye have heard that it was said by them of old time, Thou shalt not commit adultery: **28** But I say unto you, That whosoever looketh on a woman to lust after her hath committed adultery with her already in his heart.

This principle applies to women as well.

You may need to formulate additional boundaries to enable you to live a successful Christian life.

Remember to allow your Boundary List to be a living document. In other words, revisit it and make additions and subtractions as you see necessary. It is impossible for you to create such a list and account for all that you will be confronted with. Let good counsel and experience forge your boundaries.

Jesus gave us some boundaries:

Mt 5:43 ¶ Ye have heard that it hath been said, Thou shalt love thy neighbour, and hate thine enemy. **44** But I say unto you, Love your enemies, bless them that curse you, do good to them that hate you, and pray for them which despitefully use you, and persecute you;

Mt 22:37 Jesus said unto him, Thou shalt love the Lord thy God with all thy heart, and with all thy soul, and with all thy mind. **38** This is the first and great commandment. **39** And the second [is] like unto it, Thou shalt love thy neighbour as thyself. **40** On these two commandments hang all the law and the prophets.

If you are curious what law is referenced above, here it is; the ten commandments:

Exodus 20:1 ¶ And God spake all these words, saying, **2** I am the LORD thy God, which have brought thee out of the land of Egypt, out of the house of bondage. **3** Thou shalt have no other gods before me. **4** Thou shalt not make unto thee any graven image, or any likeness of any thing that is in heaven above, or that is in the earth beneath, or that is in the water under the earth: **5** Thou shalt not bow down thyself to them, nor serve them: for I the LORD thy God am a jealous God, visiting the iniquity of the fathers upon the children unto the third and fourth generation of them that hate me; **6** And shewing mercy unto thousands of them that love me, and keep my commandments. **7** Thou shalt not take the name of the LORD thy God in vain; for the LORD will not hold him guiltless that taketh his name in vain. **8** Remember the sabbath day, to keep it holy. **9** Six days shalt thou labour, and do all thy work: **10** But the seventh day is the sabbath of the LORD thy God: in it thou shalt not do any work, thou, nor thy son, nor thy daughter, thy manservant, nor thy maidservant, nor thy cattle, nor thy stranger that is within thy gates: **11** For in six days the LORD made heaven and earth, the sea, and all that in them is, and rested the seventh day: wherefore the LORD blessed the sabbath day, and hallowed it. **12** ¶ Honour thy father and thy mother: that thy days may be long upon the land which the LORD thy God giveth thee. **13** Thou shalt not kill. **14** Thou shalt not commit adultery. **15** Thou shalt not steal. **16** Thou shalt not bear false witness against thy neighbour. **17** Thou shalt not covet thy neighbour's house, thou shalt not covet thy neighbour's wife, nor his manservant, nor his maidservant, nor his ox, nor his ass, nor any thing that is thy neighbour's.

11.14

Having Fun!

This is the most important dynamic in marriage. FUN! You must have some fun! So, I decided to give you some ideas. Most of these games work great for kids too. You may consider these games too immature for you. Please remember that innocent fun is the richest. It strips away the complexity and allows you to just have fun.

GAME #1

The Laughing Game

Rules:

- The goal is to make the other person laugh for real
- The last fake laugher wins the game
- See who has the best fake laugh (Snorting is allowed)
- Funny faces with the laugh are allowed
- You cannot touch the opponent (but you can get real close)
- Talk about how smart the other person was for trying a particular face and/or laugh.

GAME #2

The Noise Game

Rules:

- The goal is to convince the other person to make the noise you are making.
- You can make a train, plane, automobile, motorcycle, gun, machine gun noise. (or animal noises)
- Even if you are terrible, you must insist that it's better than theirs.
- You get a point if you get them to make the noise.
- You get a point if they agree that yours is better.
- You get a point if they take the challenge and do a different noise.

GAME #3

The Pitch Game

Rules:

- The goal is to make your opponent laugh by changing the pitch of your voice
- Say something in a higher or lower tone than usual.
- Make it as awkward sounding as possible. If it doesn't fit, you are probably on to something!
- Challenge the other person to try it.

A friend recommended a helium balloon.

GAME #?

Try to make up your own games that you both like to play. The previous games are just to get you started.

Playing card games, board games and the such is good if you both enjoy them.

While you are doing the challenges, you might want to try the first two games to keep him guessing. He may think that you have lost your mind but you will have a great time watching him not know what to make of it. On that note, if he doesn't join you, do it anyway and watch how much fun you have watching his response. Trust me when I tell you that you are getting to him!!!

12

WHAT ABOUT THE
CHILDREN?

Most women don't have any problem dealing with children. However, I have some principles that I would like to share with you just to make sure you know them.

You are extremely influential in your children's development. There is nothing greater than a mother's love. You are not required to fix all their issues. But your willingness to be there for them will make all the difference in the world. You are a good mom when you love your children. They know you love them especially as you keep reminding them. Don't listen to your thoughts that contradict this!!!

Understand that it is your responsibility to speak into their lives; successful things. Your praise should be lavish and more often than you correct. Take an inventory of how often you praise versus correct.

In a world that will try to chew your children up and spit them out, you need to teach them how to be balanced in being tough and gentle. Teach them how to know when to be gentle and when to be tough. You hold their self-esteem in your hand. Be the one who points out the positive often. It is OK to tell them that you want them to do greater things than you have done; Jesus said that to us. Let them know that they will be great in the spiritual things of God, the emotional things and financial things.

Daughters – Hug them daily and let them know that you love them and are very proud of them. Let them know that you don't want anything to happen to them and that all you want to do is protect them from people who would try to harm them. They are expressers…so…

Sons – Hug them daily and let them know that you love them and are very proud of them. Let them know that you want to teach them how to be a real man and how to treat women.

Use your secret weapon as often as possible and you will get better responses as you raise him. If you spend time making plane, train, and automobile noises with him, you will be able to get him to come over to express himself more with you as well.

Talk with your husband on the best way to encourage them in the:

>Things of God.

>Things of the heart.

>Things of their thought life.

>Things of their talents and abilities.

>Things of their bright future.

You can talk about these things over dinner to your children.

THE POINT SYSTEM

The way I see it, it's all a point system. You take advantage of all the opportunities to gain points.

For example, you get a can of shaving cream and set it down in front of the children or child. Say Go! Grab the can, fill the shirt and splat the shirt!!! POINTS!

> **NOTE:** Don't use menthol shaving cream because it burns.... Just sayin from personal experience.

Water balloon fights.... POINTS!

Throwing the kids in the pool... POINTS!

Throwing the kids down the snow bank... POINTS!

SO, when your child has a degree in criminal justice and she can beat you in an argument, you can reply... You'll never catch me, I've got too many points!

FINALLY, AND MOST IMPORTANTLY!

Talking to your children about your spouse in a negative light will backfire on you in a BIG way. No matter what side they take, they will resent you for making them choose. This also applies to parents who are no longer in the picture or are separated from. Children, if encouraged to respect their other parents will honor you and still decide for themselves about the other. If you know the other parent is not good for the child, you will do well enforcing them to send birthday cards and respect that parent. THEY WILL DECIDE. Just don't be collateral damage because you tried to tell them the truth.

Another way to destroy your credibility with them is if you use them to get even with the other parent. Children are more perceptive than you think. If they feel that for some reason you are denying them access to the other parent, they will begin to distance themselves from you. If the other parent will not hurt the child, you should never be the reason they cannot spend time together.

13

- -

IRON SHARPENS IRON

CONFLICT AT ITS BEST

OK! You know about your Secret Weapon and hopefully you have used it to find that it gives you positive results. But maybe you slipped and went back into your old mode of operation. No problem! Just get back up and use your Secret Weapon.

The bible reads:

Proverbs 24:16 For a just [man] falleth seven times, and riseth up again: but the wicked shall fall into mischief.

You qualify to be just when you get back up! The falling is for everyone, getting back up is for the just!

THE PURPOSE OF CONFLICT

In a marriage, God uses conflict for his purposes. Not to tear you down but to smooth out some rough edges in your life. I know that you think that you are all that and a bag of chips. I definitely encourage that type of confidence. However, God wants to take you higher. The bible also reads:

Proverbs 27:17 ¶ Iron sharpeneth iron; so a man sharpeneth the countenance of his friend.

One of the ways that you know that you are smoothing a metal surface is that sparks fly. The goal here is to learn to use your secret weapon when you feel those sparks flying.

Not always are we aware of what our countenance looks like; you need your spouse to help you with that. This begs the question "What does countenance mean?"

Countenance in Hebrew is פָּנִים paniym (pronounced paw-neem') meaning presence, sight, face.

Its root word is פָּנָה panah (pronounced paw-naw') meaning to turn toward, to turn from, look, prepare, regard, and respect. Keep your countenance towards God and turn away from ungodly things. Your goal here is to resort to your secret weapon when you are upset as well as when you are not.

I know that you might be saying that this is hard. I just want to remind you that the art of learning another skill is repetition. Remember!

Phillipians 4:13 I can do all things through Christ which strengtheneth me.

14

CASE STUDIES

I have traveled the world and everywhere the Lord has allowed, I have asked wives to take these challenges to improve their influence and relationships. Some have been gracious enough to allow me to document them as case studies.

These case studies are random people that I have met and I am sharing their story with their permission. To me, they are miraculous. I hope you find encouragement from them as I do.

CASE STUDY #1

I was working in Africa when I met a woman who worked in an office on the same floor as mine. She was a Christian and we became friends. We talked about Christ, our church and our families. She was impressed that I had been married since 1984. Later she shared that their impression of Americans was that they get divorced at the drop of a hat; I confirmed this impression with other Africans.

She asked me how I have been able to stay married; I could only reply "Jesus". She said that she was a Christian and asked me if I had any pointers. At that moment, I felt led to ask her to take a challenge with me. She was cautious but willing to hear me out. I told her about the nature of Man and Woman. I shared with her the soft touch and a whisper principle. She agreed to the challenge

Challenge #1. Go home, gently touch your husband and whisper to him about you needing him to listen to relieve your stress and that it is the same effect when he thinks about things. While you are there, tell him something that you would like him to do.

> Why? Because, as warriors, men have no defense against a soft touch and a whisper.

I also shared with her that everything must be as if it is her idea. For now, she was not to share that she had been speaking with me. If he asks what is going on, she is to ask him "Can't a woman love on her husband?" He will be suspicious but will not argue with that.

Two days passed before I saw her again. When she saw me, she grabbed my hand and took me outside for privacy. She fought back the tears when she asked me: "Do you know what my husband did?". At this point I'm thinking I just created an international incident! I replied "noooo". She then said "For the first time in eleven years, he gently held me the last night.

I asked her if she requested that when she used her Secret Weapon and she replied that she did.

I told her that I was so proud of her for doing the challenge and that I knew it took deliberate effort on her part. She was so pleased with the results that I could not resist challenging her again.

I asked her if she would be willing to take on another challenge; she was less hesitant and agreed. I began to differentiate wants with needs and finished with the point – Men NEED sex.

Challenge #2. When her husband gets home, tell him that you have something very important to discuss with him in the bedroom. As you speak to him in a whisper about something you want him to know, begin taking his clothes off. If he asks you what you are doing, just tell him that you need him to know what you are saying. Then have your way with him.

> Why? Because men need to know that you desire them sexually. This type of act communicates it wonderfully.

She said that she had a boy and that she could not do that. After finding out that the he was 10 years old, I told her that she could do it. She laughed and agreed to give it a try.

A couple more days passed when she and I met again. Her feedback was very successful. When she started to remove his clothing, he asked her what she was doing but didn't stop her with a big smile on his face. She admitted that she enjoyed it immensely. I explained that the more she puts into sex, the more she will get out of it.

My real goal was what she shared next. Her husband comes home late from work occasionally without calling her and telling her. Not anymore! She was so surprised to hear him on the phone informing her what time to expect him. (This is a good time to share that he has been so affected, that he WANTS to tell her he will be late. She has hit one of his core need. He's scratching his head trying to figure out what just happened about now. Besides, she might do it again and he doesn't want to miss that!) I told her that when he gets home to gently touch him and whisper, "It was so good to hear your voice on the phone today; even though you told me you would be late getting home." She did just that!

So on to the next challenge! She was more receptive than before.

Challenge #3. When your husband gets home from work, get a towel and a pan with warm water, put a couple of drops of olive oil in the water. Kneel at his feet and wash his feet. Take the time to message them also. While doing so, tell him how much you love him and appreciate him for who he is and what he does for you. Finally, tell him that he is your king.

I explained to her that kneeling before her husband will honor him. He may give a sheepish laugh, but he won't stop you. If he tells you that you don't have to do it, tell him that you want to give him a gift from your heart. When you tell him that he is your king, he will kill himself to stay on that pedestal; all men will.

A few days later she was excited with the results. She was surprised how much she would like it and how much he loved it. During the washing, her husband wanted to know what has gotten in to her and she asked him if he liked the changes. He definitely did. By this time, she had his undivided attention. She was causing him to think about her during the day with a smile on his face.

It was then that I began to ask her:

- ❖ Do you think that you have increased in your influence with your husband? Yes!
- ❖ Do you like the changes your husband has made towards you because of your actions? Yes!
- ❖ Do you think the relationship has improved? Yes!

I continued by telling her that the most important thing to understand here is that she is more powerful in the relationship when she is gentle and loving. My next challenge was for her future.

Challenge #4. Retrain yourself to gently touch him and whisper when you are angry or emotional. This will have a dramatic effect on him. He will get it and respond much better than if you put a voice to your anger. AND, repeat the other challenges from time to time to keep him on his toes.

She agreed to work on changing how she communicates when she is upset.

CASE STUDY #2

I was in Honduras when the Lord led me to speak to a young lady who I had walked by on several occasions. When I approached her, I asked her if she was married. She said that she had been married for three years but together for seven. She also said her husband would be joining her for nine days the following weekend. I then knew what the Lord had in mind. I told her that Jesus loves her so much that he wants to show her how to improve her marriage. We spent the next hour sitting on a porch while I shared these principles with her. She agreed to use them and that she would get back with me on the results. Her situation meant that I would not be able to coach her during the process but would get with her when he had returned to the states.

Below is the email that I sent her to help her remember what to do:

> *I am so glad that we had a chance to talk. I know that you are going to have great success with your husband as he arrives today.*
>
> *Here is the BATTLE PLAN FOR PEACE!*
>
> *Rules of engagement:*
>
> 1. *You can't tell him who you've been talking to; for now. These changes are to appear as if you decided to change.*
> 2. *If he asks you what you are up to, you must reply in a whisper and gentle touch "Can't a wife love on her husband?" Smile and give him a kiss. He will be*

suspicious but he won't argue the point! You will have his attention more than ever before. Have fun!

The point here is to make him suspicious in a pleasant way. You not telling him will peak his interest. We will need his interest if you want him to read the information I have for him.

Day 1

1. *Your communication with Him will start with a gentle touch and a whisper. Try to keep it there for as many days as you can... don't give up too quickly.*

    Use this time of whispering and touching to tell him:

    a. *You deal with stress by expressing it and his listening without interrupting or suggesting anything helps you walk away from it more quickly.*

    i. *Tell him that just as he gets relief from stress by thinking about it, you get the same relief by talking about it. Women and Men were made that way.*

    ii. *Tell him that what you share may sound negative, but it is the negative things that stress you.*

    b. *What is it that you want from him that you have had difficulty telling him in the past? Tell him using a gentle touch and whisper.*

c. *"I love it when you…"*
    i. *This is VERY important! Telling him what you like when he is doing something that you don't like is very powerful.*
    ii. *Don't forget to praise him for any glimmer of effort on his part. This will encourage him to continue working on it. The art of learning is repetition.*

2. *Praise him in a whisper and a touch for all his efforts.*

    a. *This may come across to you as overboard but remember, you are practicing to change your habits as well. Besides, he is going to love it! So much that it will pull out of him a change also.*

3. *Make a point to speak to him with accolades and encouragement in anything you can find. There is nothing more powerful! You will reap great rewards; even if you are repeating yourself.*

Day 2

Wash his feet in a pan with some olive oil, if you can find some.

1. *This will require that you kneel at his feet, take his shoes and socks off, and push his pant leg up to keep them dry.*

2. *Use this time to massage his feet. Take your time.*

3. *Tell him how much you appreciate him and how grateful that you are for being his wife. Lavish him with praise and appreciation.*

4. *Dry his feet with the towel that has been on your lap.*

Day 3

Tell him that you have something very serious to talk to him about. Take him into the bedroom and as you are whispering to him about something that has nothing to do with sex, begin to take his clothes off. If he asks you what you are doing, simply tell him that you wanted to talk to him about....

1. *If he tries to take over sexually, stop him and tell him that you need him to listen to you.... You keep doing what you like with him while whispering to him. This will drive him crazy.... It's a good thing.*

2. *After sex, your way, tell him how much you really appreciated him for listening to you and that he is an awesome lover too.*

A Note on sex:

You can help him succeed with you by telling him what you like while having sex. If you want him to change, tell him what you want him to do by saying, "I like it when you..." If he doesn't change, be a little more direct by saying "I want you to ..." When he complies, let him know when he is doing good right away; this will encourage him to continue.

Every man wants to be a successful lover. You just have to teach him how to be successful with you. He also has a need to be sexually desired by his wife. This is why you must initiate the act from time to time so that he knows that you want him (VERY IMPORTANT).

Day 4

Wash his feet again in the same manner as Day 2. Then tell him while you are on your knees, "You are my King".

By this time, he will be mentally prepared to hear about our conversation and willing to read the attached document. "The Husband's Toolbox".

Also, from time to time, you will need to repeat this program to keep him on his toes. It works EVERY time.

You will have incredible influence as you learn to use the gentle touch and whisper when you are angry. This is your goal; to respond this way when you are angry. Keep working at it and you will be a pro!

Looking forward to hearing about your successful relationship!

In His Hands,

Steve Morgan
www.ForHimMinistries.net

THE RESULTS

After her husband had returned home, I asked her how it went overall. She admitted that she could not stop smiling. She continued to share. The next day, after her husband returned home, she received a text from him that was unlike any she had ever received; he gave a lot of two word texts in the past. Her husband is very conservative with money also.

Before he left, he left her $400 which was twice what she asked for. At this point, I could tell that she was a believer of the techniques. I shared that she drew this behavior out of him by her actions.

It was then that I began to ask her:

- ❖ Do you think that you have increased in your influence with your husband? Yes!
- ❖ Do you like the changes your husband has made towards you because of your actions? Yes!
- ❖ Do you think the relationship has improved? Yes!

Let me interject here that this is not for a woman to take advantage of a man. Rather to position a wife to be able to teach her husband how to love her. Men want to win at relationships and women want a good relationship. This is a win – win situation.

CASE STUDY #3

I was flying out west to attend some training for work and went to a well-known restaurant within the airport. The hostess sat me and my two other travel partners at a table for six with one woman who had already finishing her meal at the other end. We greeted her and asked her if she was alright with three men joining her. She was very friendly and said it was no problem. While eating, we engaged with her on small talk and really enjoyed her friendly disposition. About that time, I felt a spiritual drawing towards her and decided to watch to see what God had in mind.

We discovered that she was headed for the same destination and that she was on our flight as well. We then walked to the gate together. I then remember hearing the Lord say "I will be sitting next to her on the flight". Sure enough, just as we walked down the entrance ramp, she tells us what her seat was and it was right next to mine; my partners were ten rows behind us. From the ring on her hand and our conversations about our kids at the restaurant, I knew that she was married.

After we got seated, she opened up and shared that she was going home to leave her husband. I told her that I had discovered the secret weapon of a woman. She looked at me in such a way as to say that I had to tell her what it was! I began to share the Hebrew words for male and female and the different natures. I then told her about God's design in us to alleviate stress. I could see the light turn on as she commented that this all makes sense. I then shared with her the challenges and asked her if she would be willing to take them. She agreed.

Just before landing, we prayed together and I ministered to her as the Lord gave me direction. She forgave her father and she forgave herself. This relieved so much pressure that she began to cry. She collected herself before she left the plane.

We picked up our luggage as a foursome and wished her well on her journeys.

The next day, she texted me to say thank you and that she had completed the first challenge. Below is her text:

> Her: Thank you, Pastor Steve! I know He sent you to me...... Btw....step 1 complete ☺
>
> Me: Look for the smallest difference. Was it easier than you thought?
>
> Her: OK. Totally easier AND I didn't even laugh ☺
>
> Me: Lol. I'm so proud of you! You're such a brave and powerful woman! The reason why it was so easy is because it falls into your strength of being a relational being.
>
> Her: It was pretty amazing....I can't wait to see what happens with Step 2.

> Me: You will find all the challenges falling into your nester, nurture, and relational strengths. Don't forget to have fun! ☺

> Me: May I call you?

> Her: Yes.

Here is the account from her perspective over the phone.

When my husband and I met at the airport, we hugged and he noticed that I had been crying. He asked "have you been crying". I said yes and it's ok; I left it at that because the kids were with us.

When we got home, we ate and I settled into bed; I had my daughter and son with me and as we cuddled, I practiced the gentle touch and whisper with them. Both of them asked me to do it again. I was surprised that they liked it so much.

The next morning, I mentioned that I met a pastor Steve who prayed for me on the plane and God touched me. That is why I was crying last night on the plane.

Then I sat on the bed with my husband and began the first challenge:

Challenge #1 Gentle Touch and Whisper

You know how you think about things and you become silent because that's how you deal with stress? Well I have to talk about things and that is how I deal with my stress. But when you interrupt me and try to help me fix things or just interrupt me, it stops me from relieving my stress.

When I was finished, my husband began to respond with more than a two-word answer, which was very unusual mode of operation for him. He explained that it makes more sense now and that he had read something similar in another book.

When I spoke with her on her experience I shared how the gentle touch and whisper is her access into the hearts of her family.

Below is her follow-on text:

> Her: So far, so good. I told him yesterday that I was grateful to him for being such a great provider…. He said "You're so sweet!" As I touched his arm to whisper in his ear he said "That feels so good". "I really like that".

> Me: Lol. You are tapping into your Secret Weapon. Are you ready for the second challenge?

> Her: I had to look around to make sure I was talking to my husband when he said those things. LOL!!

> Her: Stoked for the 2nd Challenge ☺

> Me: OK! Remember, that it's not over until YOU say so!!!

> Her: Rodger That!

> Me: Are you having fun?

> Her: YES!!!

> Her: Didn't get to do Challenge #2 last night. I think I've got a bug. :/ I started feeling sick late afternoon yesterday.

We spoke on the phone and I told her to make him sick if she had to, but complete #2. He will be glad you did even if he got sick. (Please know that I suggested this because she was feeling better)

The text continues:

> Her: I used my Secret Weapon yesterday and forgave my husband... HUGE step for us... Things are so different now... relaxed...

> Her: Happy Wednesday Pastor Steve! Hope your day is going great

> Me: I would like to speak with you at lunch...11:30 ish. OK?

> Her: Sure

On the phone, I reminded her of the rules of engagement for the next challenge and wanted to convey to her how proud I was of her for doing these challenges. (I never promised that these would be easy)

Challenge #2 Close Encounters

The text continues:

> Her: Challenge #2 COMPLETE... It was a success... My husband was blown away!! He actually told me I

was sooo sexy AND beautiful. ☺ ... as if he was seeing me for the first time... weird but wonderful!!!

Her: This morning he said that he can't stop thinking about it!!

Me: Awesome! You touched on a core need. He will not only think about the challenge, he is being confronted with the need to know where these ideas are coming from!!!

Her: I know... he's not at all sure where I'm getting my top-secret info... HA HA HA HA!!!!

Me: He He He!!!!! ☺

Her: My reading today was Matthew, chapter 6.

Me: Good for you on the reading!

Me: Did you have fun?

Her: Best fun EVER!! He said aside from ONE other time, last night was the BEST SEX EVER, LOL!!

Me: Did you get yours?

Her: MANY TIMES, ;-)

Me: Rule of engagement: Your husband's enjoyment is side benefit. Every time you are the aggressor, it's all about you!

Her: I'm on board with that!!

Me: Are you giddy?

Her: Totally, we both are... THAT hasn't happened in YEARS!! Like we're dating and waiting to have sex, LOL!

Me: This is wonderful news!

Her: ☺

Me: I'm very proud of you for committing to challenge #2. Did you stay in charge?

Her: yes, it was killing him but he remained compliant. Hee hee!

Me: You da woman!

Me: Challenge #3 no earlier than the fifth day. Keep using your Secret Weapon... For good and bad.

Her: Got it... Challenge #3 on Saturday. I'm still using my Secret Weapon... he said today when I was using it..." You're so bad"... "you did that on purpose, but I like it".

Her: You know I was rolling on the floor with laughter ... deep down on the inside... shhhh

Me: Lol...It's great that he is confirming what I told you he would think! Some husbands just smolder over their new predicament. Lol

Her: Lol!

Me: It's still driving him curious. You are so in charge of this situation... You'll see it more clearly later.

Me: Oh yeah... Don't confirm or deny whether you did it on purpose. That comment was him fishing for info.

Me: Lol... I'm so bad!

Her: Ahhh, all right... he WAS fishing. This is WAAAAY too much fun!!!

Her: He's gettin' nada from me! I'm a vault, lol!

Me: Good!

Me: Thank you for being so transparent!

Her: Of course, ☺

Me: The ones that smolder can be hard to read... But they are just as affected by the challenge blitz.

The next day:

Me: PTL sis... Happy Friday... Wazup?

Her: Amen! We're on our way to Sedona for a day of hiking... AS A FAMILY... Whhaaatt??? Love you Pastor Steve! Sending hugs from us all ☺.

Me: You keep drawing it out of him girl!!!

Her: Lol!! I'm the one that stopped joining in on family adventures. He would take the kids by himself...This is what freedom feels like! I am free! Whom the Son sets free is free indeed!

Her: I DO feel free... it's AWESOME...we prayed together this morning... and I fell asleep on the sofa last knight, so he slept on the sofa with me...so sweet!

Me: Did you give him a trophy?

> NOTE: A trophy consists of no less than three parts. A hug, a kiss, and you looking into his eyes thanking him for .....

Me: It's never too late for a trophy.

Her: Not consciously. But after our prayer we hugged and I whispered "thank you for praying with me and I love you"

Me: That trophy was for prayer. The trophy for sleeping with you on the couch takes place when he knows it's for the act of sleeping on the couch with you.

Me: The point here is that you train him with what you like. If you want him to repeat something, then give him a trophy. Remember, a trophy impresses in his heart that you like something. He wants to win so his trophies are his guide to win with you.

Her: 10-4... I got distracted... SQUIRREL!

Her: I'll give him another trophy for the trim and one for sleeping on the sofa with me instead of waking me up.

Me: Good for you!!!! Luv ya bunches sis!

Her: Thank you!!

After the Trip:

> Me: how was your day?

> Her: We had THE BEST DAY... not an exaggeration... I've not been able to enjoy an outing with my family without feeling dread and anxiety in years... I had so much fun and I find myself smiling all the time... for no obvious reason other than I truly feel joy and happiness. For probably the first time in my entire life I KNOW GOD actually loves me too and witnessed an answered prayer when He sent an angel to me on THE DAY I was headed home to separate from my husband. I asked HIM to help me. Begged HIM send someone, anyone that I could trust to help me... I don't have family or friends that I can trust for spiritual guidance... so He sent PASTOR STEVE...

> Her: If I'm lyin', I'm dyin!!!

> Me: It is an honor to be the instrument that enables you to torment your husband! Oops, did I say that out loud? I meant love... Lol

> Her: LOL!!! Totally made me laugh out loud!!!

> Me: Me too!

> Her: Hee Hee!!!

The next day:

> Her: I'm down for the count... running fever and feeling pretty yucky. #3 will have to wait.

Me: Of course!!!! The point is to space it out to keep him guessing and not overload his heart all at once.

The next day:

Me: I hope you are feeling better.

Her: Feeling a little better... Hope you're having a blessed and relaxing day ☺

Me: Went to church and have been studying. Also, praying that you are back on your feet.

Challenge #3 Foot Washing

Her: I just completed Challenge #3.

Her: Let me just say that my hubby of one word responses was not only talkative but very open in discussing his personal feelings regarding our relationship, recent revelations about childhood events that he now realizes are affecting him... where he feels he's failed... his goals/action plan for both self-improvement and our marriage... he's actually planning a date night for Friday... he's NEVER done that. I've always been the one that had to plan date nights... which have been rare, at best.

Her: He initially felt embarrassed as I began to wash his feet... and he stated that but quickly relaxed. FYI... I did this by candlelight and used Avocado oil with essentials oils of Frankincense and Myrrh; One of his fave fragrance combinations ☺. After drying his feet, I then told him "YOU are my king". It was a bit of a difficult read for me... his expression was VERY positive, yet not one that I've seen before from him... I ended with a hug and kiss. He then asked if he could massage my feet! Pastor Steve... you KNOW I didn't pass that up!!

Her: Thank you for your prayers!

Me: Wow! Good for you!

Me: How did you feel washing his feet?

Her: Not sure How I felt...it felt nice knowing he was enjoying it and that it was a conduit for open communication.

Me: Your washing his feet was a demonstration of how you would handle his heart. At that point, he felt that he could pour out his heart to you.

Me: Are you happy with the results from your challenges?

Her: Immensely happy! This experience has been nothing short of a miracle for us!!! Yesterday was day 7 after my return. Keeping that in mind with the knowledge that we were going to separate 7 days ago definitely puts it into perspective!!! Without these Challenges, we would most likely still be separated and frustrated. We needed to see immediate results. More importantly WE NEEDED TO SEE GOD IN OUR RELATIONSHIP. These Challenges, your book, and your personal guidance and prayers have ministered to me more than anything/anyone EVER!!! I thank you...I thank HIM for answered prayer!!!

Me: Have you increased in influence in the relationship?

Her: My influence has most definitely increased.

Me: Now you can tell him with your Secret Weapon where you got this information. Tell him that you want him to read some information that has been prepared for him.

Her: I will tell him today.

Me: Give him my book, The Husband's Toolbox!

Me: Check with him on how the reading is going if he doesn't bring it up.

Me: Now it's time for Challenge #4.

Challenge #4. Retrain yourself to gently touch him and whisper when you are angry or emotional. This will have a dramatic effect on him. He will get it and respond much better than if you put a voice to your anger. AND, repeat the other challenges from time to time to keep him on his toes.

Final Thoughts

I hope that you have completed the challenges by now. If so, you have put your husbands head in "tilt" mode. At the same time, you now know how easy they are to accomplish. Additionally, you have gain a tremendous amount of influence in your relationship and he is happy about it. This is a WIN – WIN for you both.

This book is meant to be a spring board into your education about marriage and is in no way considered the final chapter. I encourage you to go to seminars and read other books on the subject. This is a progressive work in progress.

It is Jesus' will for you to be blessed in your marriage. So, I wish you Jesus.

~ Author ~

REFERENCES

Hebrew and Chaldee Lexicon to the Old Testament, Gesenius and Fürst, Boston: A.I. Bradley & Co.

James Strong, Abingdon's Strong's Exhaustive Concordance of the Bible, New Jersey, 1890 – James Strong, Key Word Comparison 1980 – Abingdon

Software: *Online Bible Edition*, Authorized Version of the King James Bible, Strong's Concordance
Version 2.00.04, June 2006

Thompson Chain Reference Study Bible King James Version, Kirkbride Bible Company, Inc. Indiana, 1988

Works by Pastor Steve Morgan

~ First Things First (What Every Christian Should Know)

Christianity is really very easy. This book shows you how scriptures make it so easy. If you are a new believer or a believer who is returning to your first love, this is for you. First Things First starts from receiving Christ into your heart and finishes with some basic principles to build on a foundation laid by the word of God. Pastor Steve also shares some personal testimonies with the principles learned that will help you avoid some of the challenges he faced as a new born again believer.

~ Second Things Second (The Doctrine of Christ)

This book covers the principles of the doctrine of Christ as mentioned in Hebrews 6:1~2. We will cover the six pillars mentioned here.

To be perfect you must stay under the grace of God. To do that you must learn more of His provisions for you. These can be found in the Doctrine of Christ. The foundation of the Doctrine of Christ is supported by six pillars which are:

- Repentance From Dead Works
- Faith Toward God
- The Doctrine Of Baptisms
- Laying On Of Hands
- Resurrection Of The Dead
- Eternal Judgment

Every Christian should be encouraged by Hebrews 6:1~2 to learn of these pillars and build a foundation that cannot be moved.

~ God's Blueprint for Spiritual Growth and Reward
(The Mosaic Tabernacle)

There are many examples of how we are to grow in God's likeness. The Tabernacle, built under the supervision of Moses, is also a map to maturity. Here you will learn some of the depths of God and His commitment to maintaining a relationship with you.

~ The Wife's Secret Weapon

Relationships are very easy but they require special tools you already have. With this book, you will learn about your "Secret Weapon". This "Secret Weapon will empower you to reach your husband emotionally deeper than ever before. You will learn how to get past the WALL that seems to frustrate you when you speak to your spouse. He will actually respond to you like a real human being! Can you imagine him talking to you in more than a few words at a time? This book will show you how to draw this person out. He really is your perfect man! When you have accomplished all the challenges in this book, you will have increased in influence in the marriage by 100-fold. This is the latest information on communicating across gender lines. If you wish that you could get your point across to the opposite sex, this book gives you what you need to succeed while having fun doing it. You won't believe how powerful these tools are until you try them!

~ The Husband's Toolbox

Relationships are really very easy, but they require special tools you already have. With this book, you will learn how to use them to their full benefit. You will also discover why your wife is the way she is and how to work with her as you were designed by God! You will learn how to make sure she never wants to leave your side. After completing the challenges in this book, you will have obtained your rightful position as the Man of your house. This is the latest information on communicating across gender lines. If you wish that you could get your point across to the opposite sex, this book gives you what you need to succeed! You won't believe how powerful these tools are until you try them!

PASTOR STEVE MORGAN's CREDENTIALS

Alumni of Sonship School of the Firstborn
Bishop Nathaniel Holcomb
Covenant Connections International (CCI)
Kaleen, TX

Master's in Business Administration (MBA)
Troy University
Troy, AL

Bachelor of Arts in Business Management
Ashford University
Clinton, IA

Associates in Applied Science in Human Relations
Community College of the Air Force (CCAF)

Associates in Applied Science in Electronic
Engineering Technology, CCAF

Pastor Steve is the founder and president of For Him Ministries. He has performed as a stand-in pastor for several churches in Germany and in Florida; allowing for vacations and smooth transitions respectively. He has been used as a consultant for churches in all auxiliaries to further the work of Christ. Pastor Steve has preached all over the globe to include: Afghanistan, Africa, Czechoslovakia, Honduras, Germany, Pakistan and the United States.

Pastor Steve also served 33 years combined in the US Air Force active duty and reserves.

He can be contacted by email at:
CustomerCare@ForHimMinistries.net
www.ForHimMinistries.net